The 74th
Art Directors
Annual and
Ninth Annual
International
Exhibition

The 74th
Art Directors
Annual and
Ninth Annual
International
Exhibition

Editor
Myrna Davis

Art Director/Graphic Design
Cara Galowitz

Associate Editors
Antje Lenthe Arcia
Mary Fichter

Copy Editors
Laura Morris
Jennifer Knox White

Production Liaison
Fiona L'Estrange

Jacket Design
Woody Pirtle, Pentagram

Exhibition Director
Luis De Jesus

Published in 1995 by
RotoVision SA
Route de Suisse 9,
CH-1295 Mies/VD,
Switzerland

The Art Directors Club, Inc.
250 Park Avenue South,
New York, New York 10003-1402,
U.S.A.

ISSN: 0735-2026
RotoVision SA ISBN: 2-88046-244-4
Watson Guptill ISBN: 0-8230-6402-6

Distribution in the United States and Canada by
Watson Guptill Publications
1515 Broadway,
New York, New York 10036,
U.S.A.

International distribution by
RotoVision SA
Route de Suisse 9,
CH-1295 Mies/VD,
Switzerland

Production and color separation in Singapore by
Provision Pte Ltd
Tel: (65) 334-7720
Fax: (65) 334-7721

Printed in Singapore

TABLE OF CONTENTS

I once picked a dye-transfer print of Irving Penn's elegant New York Still Life, *1947 out of the art department trash bin. That's how it is with commerce: once art has served its purpose, it can be lost forever. Most of the work you will see in this book is ephemeral. That is why the Annual, published continuously for three-quarters of a century, has become so useful to professionals and students of the graphic arts.*

The first exhibition of advertising art was hung in 1908 by the National Arts Club in New York. One review said the work "would surprise a good many people who had not realized that there was so much good designing in advertising." It was not until 1920, when the Art Directors Club established its annual exhibition, that such work would be preserved.

W. H. Beatty wrote in the sixth Annual, "Who knows, perhaps when a future historian of this American scene has relegated such things as business profits, quotas, and earnings to footnotes . . . it will be bits of pageantry like this that will appeal to him as saying, 'I guess they were just about like that on December 5th, 1927.'"

This, then, is just about the way we were in 1994.

—Carl Fischer
President, The Art Directors Club

1972

M. F. Agha
Lester Beall
Alexey Brodovitch
A. M. Cassandre
René Clark
Robert Gage
William Golden
Paul Rand

1973

Charles Coiner
Paul Smith
Jack Tinker

1974

Will Burtin
Leo Lionni

1975

Gordon Aymar
Herbert Bayer
Cipes Pineles Burtin
Heyworth Campbell
Alexander Liberman
L. Moholy-Nagy

1976

E. McKnight Kauffer
Herbert Matter

1977

Saul Bass
Herb Lubalin
Bradbury Thompson

1978

Thomas M. Cleland
Lou Dorfsman
Allen Hurlburt
George Lois

1979

W. A. Dwiggins
George Giusti
Milton Glaser
Helmut Krone
Willem Sandberg
Ladislav Sutnar
Jan Tschichold

1980

Gene Federico
Otto Storch
Henry Wolf

1981

Lucian Bernhard
Ivan Chermayeff
Gyorgy Kepes
George Krikorian
William Taubin

1982

Richard Avedon
Amil Gargano
Jerome Snyder
Massimo Vignelli

1983

Aaron Burns
Seymour Chwast
Steve Frankfurt

1984

Charles Eames
Wallace Elton
Sam Scali
Louis Silverstein

1985

Art Kane
Len Sirowitz
Charles Tudor

1986

Walt Disney
Roy Grace
Alvin Lustig
Arthur Paul

1987

Willy Fleckhaus
Shigeo Fukuda
Steve Horn
Tony Palladino

1988

Ben Shahn
Bert Steinhauser
Mike Tesch

1989

Rudolph de Harak
Raymond Loewy

1990

Lee Clow
Reba Sochis
Frank Zachary

1991

Bea Feitler
Bob Gill
Bob Giraldi
Richard Hess

1992

Eiko Ishioka
Rick Levine
Onofrio Paccione
Gordon Parks

1993

Leo Burnett
Yusaku Kamekura
Robert Wilvers
Howard Zieff

1994

Alan Fletcher
Norman Rockwell
Ikko Tanaka
Rochelle Udell
Andy Warhol

1995

Robert Brownjohn
Paul Davis
Roy Kuhlman
Jay Maisel

Richard Wilde
Selection Chairperson

Allan Beaver
Ed Brodsky
William H. Buckley
Lou Dorfsman
Carl Fischer
Steven Heller
Walter Kaprielian
Andrew Kner
Martin Solomon

Our industry, which is promotional by nature, has often neglected to promote itself. The Art Directors Hall of Fame takes a leadership position in recognizing and chronicling the contributions of those exceptional talents who have shaped the visual language of our culture.

Nomination for this honor is acknowledgement of lifetime achievement in the field of visual communications. Each of these laureates has demonstrated the ability to discern the difference between the ordinary and the excellent, a strong sense of ethical responsibility, and an aesthetic that has served to define and describe our times and raise the accepted standards of excellence.

—Richard Wilde
Selection Chairperson, Hall of Fame Committee

Paul Davis's restless nature—which reveals itself in the variety of visual approaches and problems he has chosen to explore in his career as an artist, graphic designer, and art director—may trace its origins to his pioneer ancestors. The son of a Methodist preacher from Texas and grandson of a Kansas newspaper man, Davis grew up in various small towns in the West and Southwest before attending Will Rogers High School in Tulsa. His art teacher there, Hortense Bateholts, was the first person to tell the young Davis he might be able to make a living as an artist. More encouragement came at the age of 17, when he won a full scholarship to the School of Visual Arts and moved to New York. His work was noticed by Art Paul, art director of Playboy, *and merited him some assignments even before graduation. In 1959, six months out of art school, Davis joined the very influential Push Pin Studios, spending three years there before leaving to begin his free-lance career.*

Davis's discoveries and enthusiasms of those years included early American painting, the works of René Magritte and the Surrealists, artists of the early Italian Renaissance, and Jasper Johns's stunning target paintings, which coalesced into a style distinctively his own in a seminal series of paintings and portraits on wood completed in the early 1960s. Employing the vocabulary and techniques of his influences, Davis borrowed from popular media such as old postcards and etchings. Jerome Snyder of Graphis *observed, "One of the persistent strengths of Davis's art is its independence of any prevailing faddishness or stylistic trends . . . The durability of {his} prodigious output rests on more permanent pillars."*

Soon after Davis opened his own studio in 1963, his work began to be published in most major magazines of the period, including Audience, Esquire, Horizon, Life, Look, McCall's, Monocle, Ramparts, Redbook, Show, Sports Illustrated, *and* Time. *Davis's style was a marked departure in the field, and paved the way for an entire generation of illustrators. In 1972, a young artist from Texas told him it was hard to get work from regional magazines "unless your work looked like Paul Davis." One art director, after being told that Davis would not execute a painting to his specific instructions, argued, "But I want your style."*

"A lot of people can do my style," *Davis replied.*

"You mean you want to do the thinking?" *Davis was told. "You should have been an art director!"*

In 1974, Giorgio Soavi, author and creative director of Olivetti, commissioned twelve paintings for Olivetti's yearly desk calendar. Davis produced a series of pastoral images based on his recollections and fantasies of the past. The edition was enormously successful, but did not contain any information about the artist. One Italian critic praised the paintings and determined that they were by an obscure 19th-century American painter, whose work had gone unpublished but obviously was endowed with strictly pictorial qualities. He wrote: "None other could indulge in similar descriptions, just like in the old days. He created a 'trompe l'oeil' so dear to our forefathers."

Davis's paintings were included in gallery and museum shows in New York, Paris, and Rome. After seeing Davis's portraits of animals at Galleria Il Gabbiano in Rome, Soavi noted: "With their dignified eyes gazing into our own eyes, as if staring at the eyes of their first photograph, these whimsical animals watch us, impatient to come to life."

Davis's human portraits, too, captured attention because they seemed to reflect their subjects' inner reality. His paintings of the famous and not-so-famous include many political, literary, and entertainment figures—Joan Baez, Ingrid Bergman, Jimmy Carter,

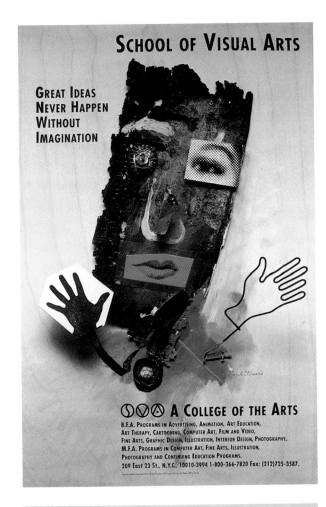

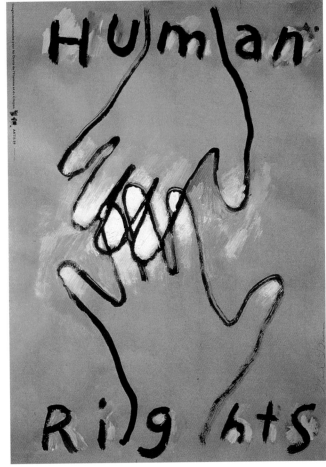

Lyndon Johnson, numerous members of the Kennedy family, Timothy Leary, Jack Nicholson, George Orwell, Ronald Reagan, and Meryl Streep, among them. His first famous poster, a romantic portrait of Che Guevera for Evergreen Review, aroused such a strong reaction when it appeared around New York City in 1967 that many copies were defaced and the magazine's offices were bombed by Cuban dissidents. By the same token, the piece became an enduring icon of the period.

Throughout the 1970s and 1980s, Davis's work became familiar to New Yorkers through entertainment posters on buses, subway platforms, and city walls. Kurt Vonnegut once wrote, "{Davis's} work is the face of the city at its best to an amazing degree." In 1987, a special Drama Desk Award was created to honor him for his theater posters.

Davis served as art director for Joseph Papp's New York Shakespeare Festival from 1985 until the producer's death, and was founding art director for the American Museum of the Moving Image in Queens and for the magazines Normal and Wigwag. Many public and private collections around the world house his paintings and posters; his 1976 Three Penny Opera poster, for instance, is in the permanent collection of the Museum of Modern Art, New York.

In the mid-1970s, the first of three major retrospectives of Davis's paintings was presented in Kamakura, Kyoto, and Gunma, Japan, and at the opening of the Centre Georges Pompidou in Paris. A 1987 retrospective included more than 180 paintings, drawings, and posters, and another in 1989, of 85 posters, toured throughout Japan. In 1990, Davis received an honorary Doctor of Fine Arts degree from his alma mater, the School of Visual Arts, where he also teaches; the coveted Medal from the American Institute of Graphic Arts, upon whose board he later served; and the Lifetime Achievement Medal in Visual Arts from the American Academy of Arts of Guild Hall, East Hampton.

Ever interested by the chance to experiment, Davis acquired his first computer in 1988 and eventually taught workshops at Kodak's short-lived Center for Creative Imaging in Camden, Maine. He still refuses to confine himself to a single style. "Sometimes a stick figure can express the human form more eloquently than a skillfully modeled drawing or a photo-realistic painting," he once said. "I don't believe that one is inherently more truthful than another."

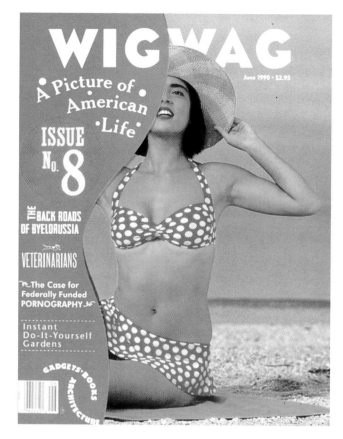

Pursuing his childhood dream to become the next Rembrandt, Roy Kuhlman studied at the Chouinard Art Institute in Los Angeles and, after moving to New York in 1946, the Art Students League; but after a number of years he realized he was looking for something else. This he found when he ran into Arnie Copeland, a friend from California who had just become art director at Lockwood Studios. Copeland introduced Kuhlman to Lockwood's bull pen as a troubleshooter and pasteup expert. Knowing practically nothing, "except on which side to smear the rubber cement," Kuhlman proved a quick study and soon lived up to his presumed reputation. At night, he taught a basic design course at the School of Advertising and Editorial Art, alongside such professionals as Eugene Carlin and Jerome Snyder.

Another big break came for Kuhlman when he was offered a job at Sudler & Hennessy, where he worked with Carl Fischer, Art Ludwig, and Ernie Smith, as well as the consummate designer and teacher Herb Lubalin. In 1954, Neil Fujita asked him to take over his position at Columbia Records. There, he gradually pooled a staff of young designers such as Ivan Chermayeff and Al Zalon, producing some of the period's most innovative work.

One year later, Kuhlman was hired by Ruder and Finn to establish an in-house art department. The budget was low and the graphic pieces sent out were small in number. Kuhlman worked with Ed Brodsky, and together they began to gain recognition until Kuhlman felt it was time to move on and try his hand at something new.

Having decided to go out on his own, Kuhlman rented a studio above Fischer's, on East 54th Street. Influenced by his friend's photographic skills, Kuhlman began solving design challenges with photography. This led to an introduction to Bill Buckley at Benton & Bowles, who gave Kuhlman the most challenging assignment of his career up to that time — the famous IBM series "Mathematics Serving Man," which won the AIGA Best Ads of the Year Award in 1958.

Although Kuhlman cites Alvin Lustig and Paul Rand as influences, it was the Abstract Expressionists, particularly the "strong, simple" style of Franz Kline, that truly inspired him. Kuhlman was one of the first to apply Abstract Expressionist ideas to design. His approach was loose, spontaneous, and serendipitous, and he worked quickly and instinctively. Because he felt there was a loss of quality if art was resized, he prepared comps in the same size as the final mechanical. Kuhlman developed a graphic language of his own, and anything within reach became part of the developing visual pastiche: old engravings, the insides of bank envelopes, his own photography, photograms, Zipatone sheets and collages, and odd pieces of letterpress type left over from other jobs.

In 1962, Kuhlman entered the movie industry. His film colleagues at Elektra Films, Jack Goodford and Lee Savage, described him as "the first film primitive." After two years, he returned to "motionless" graphics, as creative director in charge of corporate literature and sales promotion at U.S. Plywood, where he remained for almost five years. Then, on a recommendation from Kuhlman's friend Henry Wolf, IBM invited Kuhlman to create an educational seminar on the concepts and technologies behind the development and the future of the computer. In three years, he produced 700 slides and 52 live-action and animated 35-mm shorts. After this challenge, Kuhlman decided to concentrate on special effects for film animation. Just as he completed his sample reel, video special-effects generators made his newly acquired skills redundant, and he chose to retire. "In this business, if you have a ten-year life span, you're lucky — mine lasted

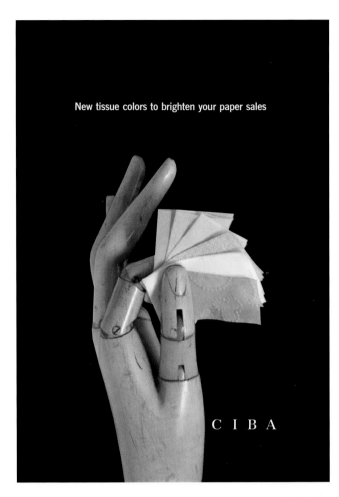

New tissue colors to brighten your paper sales

C I B A

The Ravishing of Lol Stein
a novel by Marguerite Duras

MATHEMATICS SERVING MAN

Four thousand years ago, the gifted people along the Nile had already learned that mathematics could solve many problems. With rule-of-thumb formulas and such simple tools as knotted ropes and measuring sticks, the Egyptians could determine the corner angles of a pyramid, the slope of the face, the bricks needed for a ramp. Today our tools include sensitive instruments and precise machines, but measurement remains one of the most important uses of mathematics. And the adventurous young people who become tomorrow's mathematicians will face new and exciting measurement problems as man explores outer space.

IBM.

INTERNATIONAL BUSINESS MACHINES CORPORATION

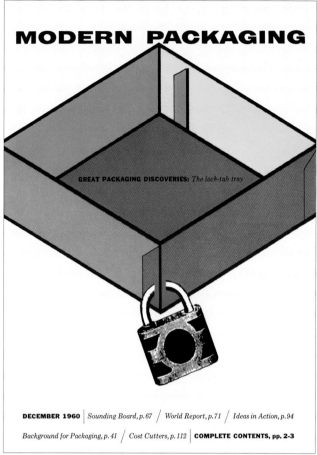

MODERN PACKAGING

GREAT PACKAGING DISCOVERIES: *The lock-tab tray*

DECEMBER 1960 | *Sounding Board, p. 67* / *World Report, p. 71* / *Ideas in Action, p. 94*

Background for Packaging, p. 41 / *Cost Cutters, p. 112* | **COMPLETE CONTENTS, pp. 2-3**

The Spanish Inn
a novel by Jean Louis Bergonzo

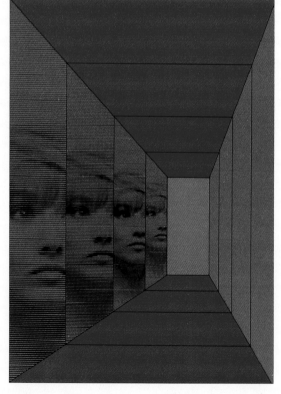

Krapp's Last Tape
and other dramatic pieces
by Samuel Beckett

EVERGREEN ORIGINAL E-226 $1.95

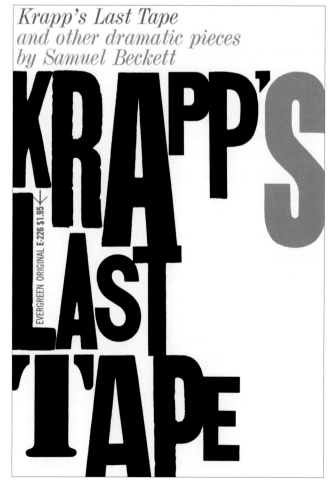

KRAPP'S LAST TAPE

35 years."

One of Kuhlman's fondest memories of his career took place in 1951, in a small Greenwich Village office of Grove Press, the fledgling publishing company that eventually brought to national prominence the writers, art, and artists of the avant-garde. He showed his portfolio of illustrations and comps, "mostly bad black-and-white photos, clumsy type, mostly sans-serif," to publisher Barney Rosset, who was not impressed. Just as Kuhlman was about to close the portfolio, Rosset caught a glimpse of doodles Kuhlman had been planning to show to record companies. When Rosset, who numbered among his friends Willem de Kooning, Kline, and Jackson Pollock, saw them, he said emphatically, "This is what I want."

For the next twenty years, Kuhlman produced some of his most brilliant work for Grove Press. His designs were the perfect counterpoint to the texts Rosset was publishing. Story of O, the erotic novel by Henry Miller, for example, was packaged in a plain white jacket to camouflage what was inside. After Grove — the first to publish third-world titles in the United States — began publishing foreign titles in 1966, Kuhlman produced such covers as The Brave African Huntress *by Amos Tutuola and* The No Plays of Japan *by Arthur Waley, which demonstrate his ability to reach both conceptual and abstract solutions. Rosset rejected only a few cover ideas. "I usually had five seconds to get a yes or no from Rosset. So, I walked slowly across the office toward Rosset's desk, holding the comp up so he'd have some {extra} time to look at it," Kuhlman says, adding, "Barney was the greatest client I ever had. He gave me the freedom to explore, to fail, and to win."*

Jay Maisel finds beauty in a thousand places—some whose association with beauty is incongruous, all where there was beauty to begin with. The distinctive light and gesture in Maisel's vibrant photographs, which set them apart from the work of other photographers, have earned their creator a reputation of excellence. By the time Maisel was 24 years old, he was given a solo show at Photographers Gallery in New York. Yet it took at least five years more before Maisel would admit to being a photographer.

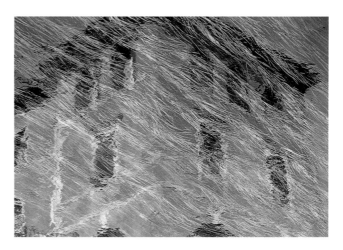

Maisel became interested in the visual arts at an early age. He concentrated on graphic design in high school, and after graduation studied privately with painter Joseph Hirsch. He spent the next three years at Cooper Union in New York, where he studied painting, drawing, architectural design, and calligraphy. Maisel's interest in painting and graphics then led him to Yale University and, there, to Bauhaus master Josef Albers. Although Maisel was at the top of Albers's class in color perception, his restless personality was incompatible with the pace of painting. Morris Kantor, a teacher, concurred, describing Maisel's paintings as "emotional outbursts."

At Yale, working with a group of student artists and architects and philosopher/engineer Buckminster Fuller, Maisel chanced to use a camera seriously for the first time. While his only formal photography instruction was a class with Herbert Matter, he absorbed Andreas Feininger's Introduction to Photography *and found himself sneaking off to take pictures when he was supposed to be painting and drawing. It is not surprising that his photographs have been described as "painterly" and compared to the work of J. M. W. Turner and Andrew Wyeth.*

Before becoming a free-lance photographer for major advertising agencies and corporations in the United States and abroad, Maisel photographed extensively on his own. At the age of 25, he decided to see every art director at BBDO and sat in their offices every day for weeks. With no luck there, he moved on to J. Walter Thompson. Finally, after a month, his patience paid off and he received his first assignment. Once home, he looked at his portfolio, reread the requisition, then looked at his portfolio again. The agency wanted him to shoot a woman lifting a curtain in a studio, yet his entire portfolio consisted of outdoor shots using available light. He had no idea how to use lighting. Approaching crisis point, he recalled a lesson Alexey Brodovitch had taught him: "Do the assignment for yourself even if you're doing it for them; do it for yourself as well as for them." With that in mind, Maisel made the client wait a week and a half until the available light was right.

Choice and selection, rather than imposition and manipulation, are the hallmarks of Maisel's philosophy. He does not believe in manipulating the image either before or after he releases the shutter. When asked by Pete Turner—famous for his imaginative use of filters—how he achieved such fantastic lighting effects without polarizers or filtration, Maisel replied, "I wait."

Maisel takes many of his personal photos while on assignment for corporations, and sells dye transfers to private collections. A Maisel photograph seen in a gallery may also show up in a commercial work. "He doesn't make a distinction between art and commercial work," says friend and artist Joel Meyerowitz, "and probably Rubens didn't make a distinction, either, when he made things for himself and when he made things on commission. Jay's biggest following and celebrity is in the world of commercial photography, and he is revered there as a real heavyweight professional with a great appetite and an engaging eye."

John Morrison, an art director for Campbell-Mithun in

Minneapolis, once accompanied Maisel to photograph Winnebago motor homes in North Dakota and was "a little concerned because of the photographer's 'superstar status.' I thought, 'Does he really want to go to North Dakota and shoot motor homes? Will I be getting the back of his hand?'" Not only did Maisel shoot from 4 a.m. to 11 p.m. for six days straight, but Morrison insists that Maisel must have influenced the very weather. "That week we had glorious sunrises, sunsets, a thunderstorm. I told him, 'I've never seen this kind of light before,' and Jay said, 'It's always around. You just don't see it.'"

Maisel has taught at the School of Visual Arts, and at Cooper Union from 1969 to 1974. His work has been recognized with awards from, among others, Cooper Union, The Art Directors Club, The American Society of Media Photographers, Syracuse, and the International Center of Photography, New York, and with solo exhibitions at Cooper Union, the International Center of Photography, The Silver Image Gallery, the Alternative Center for International Arts, and the Space Gallery, which he co-founded with Ernst Haas and Turner in 1977 in New York when none of the city's galleries were showing color photography.

Maisel continues to teach young photographers at workshops, seminars, and lectures around the world and in his studio, a six-story former bank building on the Bowery in New York. Visitors are ushered onto an indoor basketball court, entrance to the domain of a self-described "pack-rat collector" who readily admits to having "the soul of a janitor." The Bank is filled with his photographs and "esoteric aesthetica."

For over 30 years, Maisel's unique images have made people stop and look—a horizontal shot of the Eiffel Tower for United Technologies Corporation; a scorching sun in a brilliant red sky for Carrier air conditioners; a stunningly red car hood for Inmont paint. In each, copy is minimal, the advertisement relying on the photograph to make its point. Maisel has used a surreal image of helicopters, shot for a Sikorsky spread, as his own promotional piece. He gives the same meticulous attention to both his commercial and his personal work. Maisel tells his students, "If you're really lucky, you can structure your work, on rare occasions, to where you're doing exactly what you would like to do. Which is to wander around, blindly looking for things, without any preconceived notion. That's the way I like to do it."

GOLD AND SILVER MEDALISTS

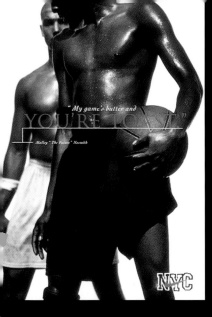

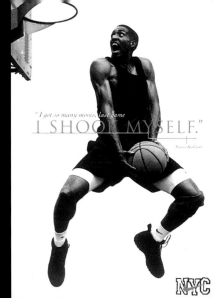

"My game's butter and **YOU'RE TOAST.**"

Malloy "The Future" Nesmith

" I got so many moves, last game **I SHOOK MYSELF.**"

Pearce Kirkland

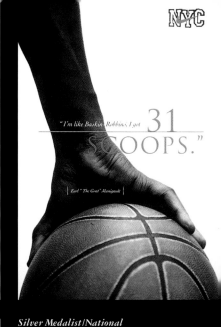

"I'm like Baskin-Robbins, I got **31 SCOOPS.**"

Earl "The Goat" Manigault

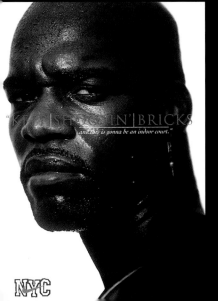

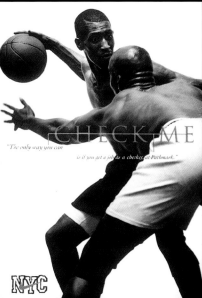

"KEEP SHOOTIN' BRICKS *and this is gonna be an indoor court.*"

"The only way you can **CHECK ME** *is if you get a job as a checker at Pathmark.*"

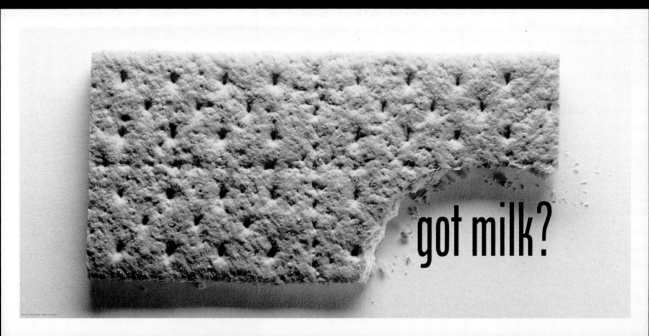

Silver Medalist/National

TRANSIT, CAMPAIGN
Got Milk?
ART DIRECTORS *Rich Silverstein, Peter di Grazia*
CREATIVE DIRECTORS *Jeffrey Goodby,*
Rich Silverstein
DESIGNER *Chuck McBride*
PHOTOGRAPHER *Terry Heffernan*
PRODUCER *Michael Stock*
FOOD STYLIST *Marilee Hague*
AGENCY *Goodby, Berlin and Silverstein*
CLIENT *California Fluid Milk Processor*
Advisory Board

Gold Medalist/International

GENERAL, SINGLE
The 200th Anniversary of Sharaku
ART DIRECTOR *Mitsuo Katsui*
DESIGNER *Mitsuo Katsui*
AGENCY *PARCO*
CLIENT *The Mainichi Newspapers*

Gold Medalist/International

GENERAL, SINGLE
PREXCEED "HFX"
ART DIRECTOR *Koji Mizutani*
CREATIVE DIRECTOR *Tamotsu Kawashima*
DESIGNERS *Masashi Yamashita, Hiroshi Ohmizo*
COPYWRITER *Kazushi Shimoda*
PHOTOGRAPHER *Sachiko Kuru*
AGENCY *Dentsu, Inc.*
STUDIO *Mizutani Studio*
CLIENT *Yanagiya Co., Ltd.*

注意、要ス。

注意、要ス。

YOU MAY HAVE HEARD THAT THERE ARE STARVING CHILDREN IN CHINA. MAYBE IT'S BECAUSE WE HIRED AWAY THEIR BEST CHEF.

HUNAN GARDEN 湖南園

11532 PAGE SERVICE RD. 314.432.7015

WHICH WOULD YOU RATHER HAVE AT OUR RESTAURANT, GOOD ENGLISH OR GOOD CHINESE?

HUNAN GARDEN 湖南園

11532 PAGE SERVICE RD. 314.432.7015

SAVE A ROT AT ONE OF ST. ROUIS' MOST DERICIOUS RESTAURANTS.

HUNAN GARDEN 湖南園

11532 PAGE SERVICE RD. 314.432.7015

Silver Medalist/National

GENERAL, CAMPAIGN
Rots and Rots
ART DIRECTOR *David Nien-Li Yang*
COPYWRITERS *Eric Weltner, Rich Wolchock,*
David Nien-Li Yang
AGENCY *The Puckett Group*
CLIENT *Hunan Garden Restaurant*

Silver Medalist/International

GENERAL, CAMPAIGN
Mujirushi-Ryohin Clothing Posters
ART DIRECTOR *Masaaki Hiromura*
BRAND DIRECTORS *Ikko Tanaka, Kazuko Koike*
DESIGNERS *Masaaki Hiromura, Toshiyuki Kojima*
COPYWRITER *Yoichi Umemoto*
PHOTOGRAPHER *Takashi Oyama*
CLIENT *Ryohin-Keikaku Co., Ltd.*

Silver Medalist/International

GENERAL, CAMPAIGN
In the Course of Nature
ART DIRECTOR *Andrei Shelutto*
CREATIVE DIRECTORS *Andrei Shelutto,*
Igor Gurovich
DESIGNERS *Andrei Shelutto, Igor Gurovich*
COPYWRITER *Roman Frolov*
PHOTOGRAPHER *Eduard Basilija*
AGENCY *IMA Press Publishers*
CLIENT *IMA-Press Association*

МЫ В НАТУРЕ

В NATURE

МЫ В НАТУРЕ

Silver Medalist/National

COMMERCIAL, 30 SECONDS OR LESS
Sound Toner
ART DIRECTOR *Jerry Gentile*
CREATIVE DIRECTOR *Steve Rabosky*
COPYWRITER *Scott Vincent*
PRODUCER *Michelle Burke*
DIRECTOR *Jeff Gorman*
AGENCY *Chiat/Day Inc. Advertising*
CLIENT *Sunkist California Pistachios*

VISUAL: *Open on August Priest doing various sweeping arm motions around a man with his back to Priest.*
INTERVIEWER: *So what does sound toning do?*
VISUAL: *Close-up of man, August Priest.*
PRIEST: *It opens your heart chakra, so you feel unconditional love just vibrating throughout all of you. Comfortably and easily. You can feel your guardian angel surrounding you. Creating balance and harmony.*
SUPER: *August Priest, Sound Toner.*
VISUAL: *Cut to Priest and Dan McLoughlin standing. Priest sound toning into Dan's back.*
SFX: *Sound-toning noises.*
FADE TO SUPER: *Everybody knows the best nuts come from California.*
VISUAL: *Cut to product shot of pistachio bag crashing.*
ANNCR. VO: *Sunkist California Pistachios. Now that's a nut.*
SUPER: *California Pistachios.*

EVERYBODY KNOWS THE BEST NUTS COME FROM CALIFORNIA.

CALIFORNIA PISTACHIOS

Gold Medalist/National

COMMERCIAL, 30 SECONDS OR LESS, CAMPAIGN
Soul, Fighting Fruit, 30 Seconds
ART DIRECTORS *Mike Rosen, Ducan Milner*
CREATIVE DIRECTOR *Marty Cooke*
COPYWRITER *Marty Cooke*
PRODUCERS *Peter Cline, Andrew Chinich*
DIRECTOR *Greg Ramsey*
MUSIC *Kate Bush*
AGENCY *Chiat/Day, New York*
CLIENT *Fruitopia*

ADDITIONAL AWARD

Silver Medalist
COMMERCIAL, 30 SECONDS OR LESS
30 Seconds

Soul
SUPER: *This is what Citrus Consciousness™ can do to your tongue. Imagine what it can do for your soul. Fruitopia™ from Minute Maid®. For the (mind/icon, body/icon, planet/icon).*

Silver Medalist/National

COMMERCIAL, OVER 30 SECONDS
Faces
ART DIRECTOR *Dean Stefanides*
CREATIVE DIRECTORS *Dean Stefanides,*
Larry Hampel
DESIGNERS *Jakob Trollbeck, R/Greenberg*
Associates
COPYWRITER *Larry Hampel*
PRODUCTION COMPANY *Sandbank, Kamen &*
Partners with R/Greenberg Associates
PRODUCER *Jean Muchmore*
DIRECTOR/CINEMATOGRAPHER *Henry Sandbank*
AGENCY *Houston Effler Hampel & Stefanides*
CLIENT *NEC Technologies*

ANNCR. VO: *Multimedia is here. And NEC is
making it more powerful than ever. With
sharper monitors. Faster CD-ROM readers. And
advanced networking capabilities. NEC. See,
hear, and feel the difference.*

Gold Medalist/National

COMMERCIAL, OVER 30 SECONDS, CAMPAIGN
Press Conference, Why So Tough, I Had a Dream,
Playground/Mother, Street Dribbler
ART DIRECTORS *Jason Peterson, Paul Hirsch,*
Izzy DeBellis
CREATIVE DIRECTOR *Andy Berlin*
COPYWRITERS *Izzy DeBellis, Paul Hirsch,*
Jason Peterson
PRODUCER *Deborah Sullivan*
DIRECTOR *Jeff Priess*
AGENCY *Berlin Cameron Doyle*
CLIENT *NBA*

ADDITIONAL AWARD

Silver Medalist
COMMERCIAL, OVER 30 SECONDS
Press Conference

Street Dribbler
VISUAL: *Bill Murray dribbling basketball on city*
street at night.
MUSIC: *Dominican monk "chantlike" music.*
MURRAY: *It's like a religion with me. I believe in*
myself. I'm there for me. I believe in the ball.
The ball is there for me. I believe in the court.
But I just can't find the court. I have a ball and
I'm here...I just can't find my court. I know it's
out there...somewhere.
VISUAL: *Fade to black.*

Silver Medalist/National

COMMERCIAL, LOW BUDGET
Nike NYC Series #2, Five Spots
ART DIRECTOR *John C. Jay*
CREATIVE DIRECTORS *Dan Wieden, Jamie Barrett,*
Jim Riswold
COPYWRITER *Jimmy Smith*
PRODUCERS *Renee Raab, Radical-Media*
DIRECTOR *Robert Leacock*
AGENCY *Wieden & Kennedy*
CLIENT *Nike*

Trash Talk
Then I bring it back out cause I wanna
embarrass him. I wanna shake him and fake
him, and I'm lookin' at his face sayin' whatcha
want me to do, make a lay-up, make a jump
shot? Make up your mind whatcha want me to
do. Bam bam bam, I'm goin' through my legs
twice, then I'm gonna reverse, hesitate, stop. I
freeze, then I pull up on him, then I back up on
him. "Yeah, c'mon nah nah nah uh oh, you ain't
guardin' me, oh here I'm back again, oh I thought
you was guardin' me." An' I'm sayin', "Now let's
go, push up, push up, push up now." Up, he's in
the air, I done faked him, but I goin' back and
fake him again, and I goin' to the basket, layin'
it up, behind my back double reverse fake head
fake, I'm lookin' at him sayin', "Hey you can't
guard me man, I got so many moves last game I
shook myself."

Silver Medalist/National

FULL PAGE OR SPREAD
Absolut Brooklyn Bridge
ART DIRECTORS *Dan Braun, Bart Slomkowski*
CREATIVE DIRECTORS *Arnie Arlow, Peter Lubalin*
COPYWRITERS *Dan Braun, Bart Slomkowski*
PHOTOGRAPHER *Steve Bronstein*
AGENCY *TBWA Advertising, Inc.*
CLIENT *Absolut*

ABSOLUT BROOKLYN.

Michael/Sandy

SFX: *Crackle of answering machine.*

SFX: *Beep.*

SANDY: *This is to Michael. I love you more than anything in the world. And you destroyed your life...you destroyed our lives...you took away everything that we had and we loved...and you're going to kill yourself and you won't listen to nobody and I don't want to see that happen to you. So please wake up and go for help before something goes wrong and you'll never be able to take that...to make that step to go. I love you. Sandy.*

SFX: *Phone hangs up.*

ANNCR.: *If someone you know is using drugs, you better talk to them. And if they won't listen, talk to us. Call 212-727-8502. Leave a recording, and we'll get it on the air. 212-727-8502. Millions will hear it. Maybe one person out there will get the message. A message from The Partnership for a Drug-Free America.*

Distinctive Merit/International

OUTDOOR, CAMPAIGN
Dog Bone, Dog Collar, Dog Face
ART DIRECTOR *Michael McLaughlin*
CREATIVE DIRECTORS *Larry Tolpin,*
Michael McLaughlin, Stephen Creet
COPYWRITER *Stephen Creet*
ILLUSTRATORS *Various*
AGENCY *BBDO Canada*
CLIENT *Molson Breweries*

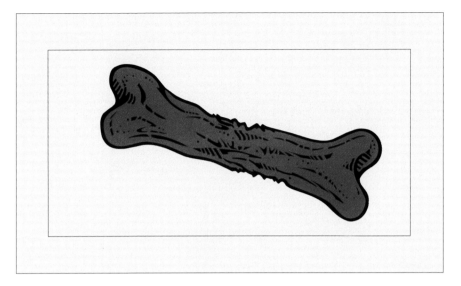

Distinctive Merit/International

OUTDOOR, CAMPAIGN
Kodak Gold D.I.A.R. Film: Yellow, Red, Blue
ART DIRECTOR *Jean-Michel Alirol*
CREATIVE DIRECTOR *Jean-Paul Bacquer*
COPYWRITER *Dominique Marchand*
PHOTOGRAPHER *Richard Croft*
ART BUYER *Elaine Harris*
AGENCY *Young & Rubicam France*
CLIENT *Kodak Pathe, Philippe Veron*

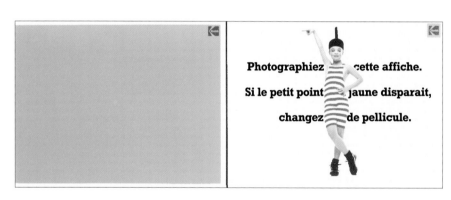

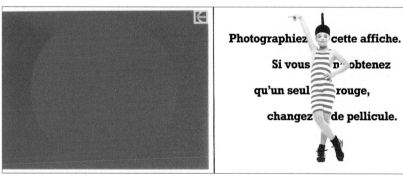

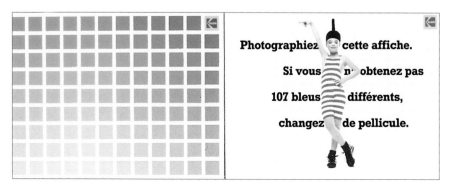

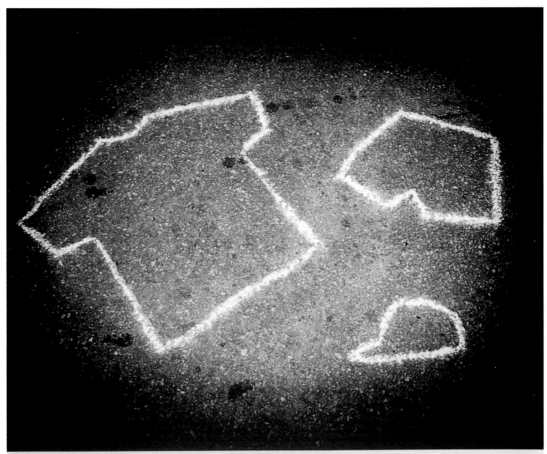

THE LOS ANGELES COUNTY CORONER'S OFFICE GIFT SHOP

1104 North Mission Road, Room 216 (213) 343-0786. Proceeds benefit the Youthful Drunk Driving Visitation Program.

To claim that only tough guys wear Everlast is probably a generalization.
However, it's doubtful many start the day with a croissant and a cup of cappuccino.

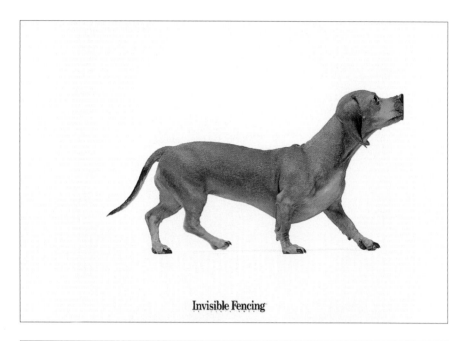

Invisible Fencing

(facing page, top)
Distinctive Merit/National

PUBLIC SERVICE, SINGLE
L.A. Coroner's Gift Shop Poster
ART DIRECTOR *Ian Barry*
CREATIVE DIRECTORS *Matt Smith, Ian Barry*
DESIGNER *Ian Barry*
COPYWRITER *Steve Dolbinski*
PHOTOGRAPHER *Abe Spear*
ILLUSTRATOR *Ian Barry*
PRODUCER *Deborah Burton*
AGENCY *Arnold Finnegan Martin*
CLIENT *Los Angeles County Coroner*

(facing page, bottom)
Distinctive Merit/National

GENERAL, SINGLE
Nails
ART DIRECTOR *Gary Goldsmith*
CREATIVE DIRECTOR *Gary Goldsmith*
COPYWRITER *Gary Goldsmith*
PHOTOGRAPHER *Steve Hellerstein*
AGENCY *Goldsmith/Jeffrey*
CLIENT *Everlast*

ADDITIONAL AWARD

Merit
GENERAL, CAMPAIGN
Nails, Biceps

Distinctive Merit/National

GENERAL, SINGLE
Invisible Fencing
ART DIRECTOR *Ian Barry*
CREATIVE DIRECTOR *Matt Smith*
DESIGNER *Ian Barry*
COPYWRITER *Steve Dolbinski*
PHOTOGRAPHER *Bryan Morehead*
ILLUSTRATOR *Davidson & Co.*
PRODUCER *Betsy Steidel*
AGENCY *Arnold Finnegan Martin*
CLIENT *Invisible Fencing, Inc.*

Distinctive Merit/National

GENERAL, SINGLE
Louise Fili, Cincinnati
ART DIRECTOR *Louise Fili*
CREATIVE DIRECTOR *Louise Fili*
DESIGNER *Louise Fili*
PHOTOGRAPHER *Ed Spiro*
STUDIO *Louise Fili Ltd.*
CLIENT *Art Directors Club of Cincinnati*

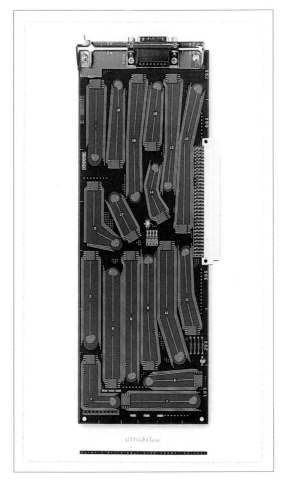

GTI Golf Classic

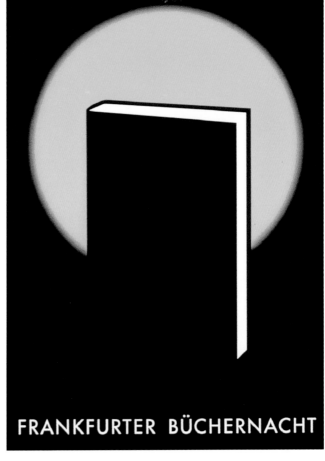

Distinctive Merit/National

GENERAL, SINGLE
Golf Outing
ART DIRECTOR *Jeff Jahn*
CREATIVE DIRECTOR *Lyle Wedemeyer*
COPYWRITER *Pete Smith*
PHOTOGRAPHER *Scott McCulley*
ILLUSTRATOR *Scott McCulley*
AGENCY *Martin/Williams, Pete Smith Advertising*
STUDIO *Parallel Productions*
CLIENT *GTI*

Distinctive Merit/International

GENERAL, SINGLE
Frankfurter Büchernacht
ART DIRECTOR *Gunter Rambow*
CREATIVE DIRECTOR *Gunter Rambow*
DESIGNER *Gunter Rambow*
ILLUSTRATOR *Gunter Rambow*
AGENCY *Rambow + van de Sand*
STUDIO *Rambow + van de Sand*
CLIENT *Frankfurter Buchhändler und Verleger*

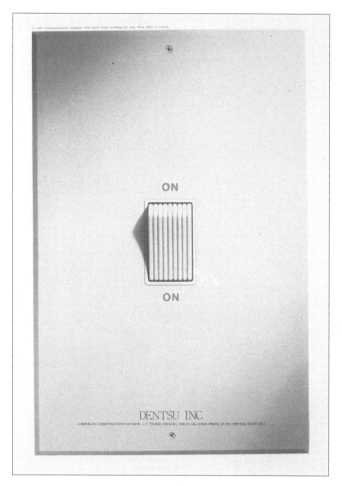

Distinctive Merit/International

GENERAL, SINGLE
A Total Communications Company That Never Stops Working
ART DIRECTOR *Takashi Fukui*
CREATIVE DIRECTOR *Masaharu Nakano*
DESIGNER *Takashi Fukui*
COPYWRITER *Marc X. Grigoroff*
PHOTOGRAPHER *Takashi Seo*
AGENCY *Dentsu, Inc.*
STUDIO *Dentsu Cotec Inc.*
CLIENT *Dentsu, Inc.*

Distinctive Merit/International

GENERAL, SINGLE
Wedding Ceremony
ART DIRECTORS *Motoya Sugisaki, Fuhmihiko Enokido*
CREATIVE DIRECTOR *Motoya Sugisaki*
DESIGNER *Motoya Sugisaki*
PHOTOGRAPHER *Toru Kinoshita*
ILLUSTRATOR *Motoya Sugisaki*
AGENCY *Motoya Sugisaki Design Office*
CLIENT *St. Sonea Chapel*

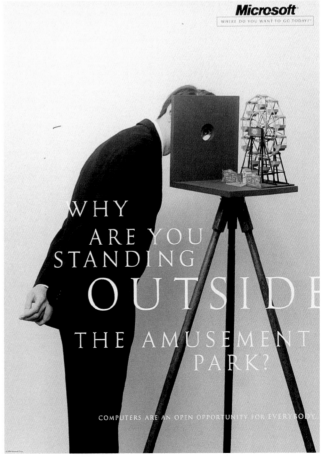

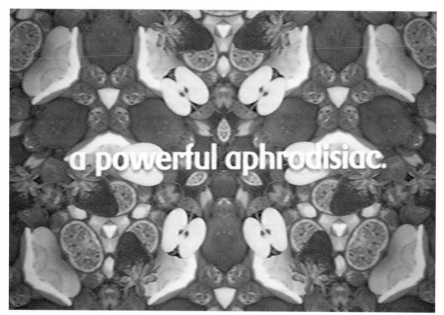

(facing page)
Distinctive Merit/National

POSTERS, GENERAL, CAMPAIGN
Where Do You Want to Go Today? P.O.S.
ART DIRECTORS *John Jay, Steve Sandstrom*
CREATIVE DIRECTOR *John Jay*
DESIGNER *Steve Sandstrom*
COPYWRITER *Jim Riswold*
PHOTOGRAPHER *Geoff Kern*
AGENCY *Wieden & Kennedy*
STUDIO *Sandstrom Design*
CLIENT *Microsoft*

(right)
Distinctive Merit/National

COMMERCIAL, 30 SECONDS OR LESS
Aphrodisiac
ART DIRECTORS *Mike Rosen, Ducan Milner*
CREATIVE DIRECTOR *Marty Cooke*
COPYWRITER *Marty Cooke*
PRODUCERS *Peter Cline, Andrew Chinich*
DIRECTOR *Greg Ramsey*
MUSIC *Kate Bush*
AGENCY *Chiat/Day, New York*
CLIENT *Fruitopia*

SUPER: *The ancient Maori believed passion fruit was a powerful aphrodisiac. Hey, it couldn't hurt. Try Strawberry Passion Awareness ™. Fruitopia ™ from Minute Maid ®. For the (mind/icon, body/icon, planet/icon).*

Distinctive Merit/National

COMMERCIAL, 30 SECONDS OR LESS
Ping Pong Lady
ART DIRECTOR *Jerry Gentile*
CREATIVE DIRECTOR *Steve Rabosky*
COPYWRITER *Scott Vincent*
PRODUCER *Michelle Burke*
DIRECTOR *Jeff Gorman*
AGENCY *Chiat/Day Inc. Advertising*
CLIENT *Sunkist California Pistachios*

VISUAL: *Open on close-up of a woman in front of a bike path.*
SFX: *Bike bell rings.*
VISUAL: *Cut to Ruth playing solo with ping pong balls, catching them in her mouth. Ruth catches ping pong balls with hand and bows. Ruth plays "Three Blind Mice" on the xylophone using the ping pong balls shooting from her mouth.*
MUSIC: *From the song "Three Blind Mice."*
FADE INTO SUPER: *Everybody knows the best nuts come from California.*
VISUAL: *Cut to product shot of pistachio bag crashing.*
ANNCR. VO: *Sunkist California Pistachios. Now that's a nut.*
SUPER: *California Pistachios.*

EVERYBODY KNOWS
THE BEST NUTS COME
FROM CALIFORNIA.

CALIFORNIA PISTACHIOS

ONE DAY NATURE
IS GOING TO LOSE RESPECT
FOR HUMAN BEINGS.

Distinctive Merit/International

COMMERCIAL, PUBLIC SERVICE
Birds
ART DIRECTORS *Luiz Claudio de Carvalho,*
Roberto Esteves
CREATIVE DIRECTOR *Clovis Calia*
COPYWRITERS *Fábio Victória, Paulo Leite*
PHOTOGRAPHER *Klaus Meewes*
PRODUCER *José Augusto Machado*
DIRECTOR *Vinicius Galcliardi*
MUSIC *MCR*
AGENCY *Standard, Ogilvy & Mathers*
CLIENT *Gazeta Television*

Distinctive Merit/National

COMMERCIAL, LOW BUDGET
Accountant
ART DIRECTOR *Robert Shaw West*
CREATIVE DIRECTOR *Mike Drazen*
COPYWRITER *Ken Cills*
PRODUCER *Joe Mosca*
AGENCY *Earle Palmer Brown, Philadelphia*
STUDIO *Earle Palmer Brown, Philadelphia*
CLIENT *WMMR 93.3 FM*

VO: *Doctors have this theory that if you play classical music to infants they'll grow up with a better understanding of complex relationships like math. They don't know what effect rock and roll will have, but I play this stuff for him anyway. I figure the world can live with one less accountant.*
SUPER: *Logo.*

Distinctive Merit/National

COMMERCIAL, LOW BUDGET
Litter
ART DIRECTOR *Peter Cohen*
COPYWRITER *Jay Taub*
PRODUCERS *Peter Cohen, Jay Taub*
DIRECTOR *Daniel Fisher*
AGENCY *StreetSmart Advertising*
CLIENT *Coalition for the Homeless*

ADDITIONAL AWARD

Merit
COMMERCIAL, PUBLIC SERVICE

SFX: *City-street sounds throughout.*
VISUAL: *Open on a busy New York City sidewalk strewn with garbage, litter, and debris. Camera dollies down sidewalk as people walk by. More litter blows through frame.*
SUPER: *Please don't litter.*
VISUAL: *Camera still dollying. We pass more debris and litter until we come across a homeless man lying on the sidewalk.*
SUPER: *People have to sleep here.*
VISUAL: *Dissolve to black.*
SUPER: *Coalition for the Homeless. 212-964-5900.*

Distinctive Merit/National

FULL PAGE OR SPREAD
Absolut D.C.
ART DIRECTOR *Maria Kostyk-Petro*
CREATIVE DIRECTORS *Arnie Arlow, Peter Lubalin*
COPYWRITERS *Lisa Retting-Falcone, Alan Levine*
PHOTOGRAPHER *Steve Bronstein*
AGENCY *TBWA Advertising, Inc.*
CLIENT *Absolut*

Distinctive Merit/National

FULL PAGE OR SPREAD
Bonnie Blair
ART DIRECTORS *Maria Kostyk-Petro, Lisa Lipkin*
CREATIVE DIRECTORS *Arnie Arlow, Peter Lubalin*
DESIGNERS *Maria Kostyk-Petro, Lisa Lipkin*
COPYWRITERS *Lisa Lipkin, Maria Kostyk-Petro*
AGENCY *TBWA Advertising, Inc.*
CLIENT *Evian*

TO YOU IT LOOKS LIKE A
HALF-EATEN RED APPLE.

TO SOMEONE WHO'S BEEN
THROUGH OUR EXHIBIT, IT
LOOKS LIKE IT WAS EATEN
BETWEEN 6 AND 12 P.M. BY
A MALE WITH A CHIPPED
UPPER-RIGHT BICUSPID,
AN EXTREME OVERBITE,
AND A MISSING LOWER
LEFT FIRST MOLAR THAT
POSITIVELY CONFIRMS THE
IDENTITY OF THE VICTIM IN
YOUR FIRST MURDER CASE.

A robbery in a diner. A dead body in the alley. Whodunit?
It's the new interactive exhibit where you hear the eye
witnesses, gather the evidence, and use the science of
forensics to crack the case. Investigation is now underway.

WHODUNIT?
MUSEUM OF SCIENCE
It's Alive!™

TO YOU IT LOOKS LIKE AN
ORDINARY BLACK COMB.

TO SOMEONE WHO'S BEEN
THROUGH OUR EXHIBIT IT
LOOKS LIKE IT BELONGED
TO A RIGHT-HANDED, CURLY
GRAY-HAIRED, MIDDLE-AGED
CAUCASIAN MALE, WHO
PARTS HIS HAIR ON THE LEFT
SIDE, IS A HEAVY SMOKER
OF BOTH CIGARETTES AND
MARIJUANA, MOST LIKELY
HAS A JOB THAT INVOLVES
WORKING WITH INDUSTRIAL
INSECTICIDES AND COULD BE
AN EXTREMLY IMPORTANT
KEY TO SOLVING YOUR
VERY FIRST MURDER CASE.

A robbery in a diner. A dead body in the alley. Whodunit?
It's the new interactive exhibit where you hear the eye
witnesses, gather the evidence, and use the science of
forensics to crack the case. Investigation is now underway.

WHODUNIT?
MUSEUM OF SCIENCE
It's Alive!™

Distinctive Merit/National

CAMPAIGN
Whodunit
ART DIRECTOR *Ron Rosen*
CREATIVE DIRECTORS *Rich Herstek, Peter Favat*
COPYWRITER *Pete Nichols*
PHOTOGRAPHER *Bruce Peterson*
AGENCY *Houston Effler Herstek Favat*
CLIENT *Museum of Science, Boston*

TO YOU IT LOOKS LIKE
A TUBE OF LIPSTICK.

TO SOMEONE WHO'S BEEN
TO OUR EXHIBIT IT LOOKS
LIKE IT BELONGED TO
A HEAVY, LEFT-HANDED,
5'10", BROWN-HAIRED
WOMAN WHO'S WANTED
IN CONNECTION WITH
TWO ROBBERIES IN
ST. PETERSBURG, FLORIDA
AND FLED TO BOSTON
FOUR MONTHS AGO AND
IS NOW ONE OF THE
PRIME SUSPECTS IN YOUR
FIRST MURDER CASE.

A robbery in a diner. A dead body in the alley. Whodunit?
It's the new interactive exhibit where you hear the eye
witnesses, gather the evidence, and use the science of
forensics to crack the case. Investigation is now underway.

WHODUNIT?
MUSEUM OF SCIENCE
It's Alive!™

Distinctive Merit/National

CAMPAIGN
EDS Management Consulting Services
ART DIRECTORS *Dick Mitchell, Leslie Davis*
CREATIVE DIRECTOR *Dick Mitchell*
DESIGNER *Dick Mitchell*
COPYWRITERS *Leslie Davis, Dick Mitchell*
PHOTOGRAPHER *Brian Fewell*
AGENCY *The Richards Group*
STUDIO *RBMM*
CLIENT *EDS*

(facing page)
Distinctive Merit/National

NEWSPAPER, PUBLIC SERVICE, FULL PAGE OR SPREAD
She Couldn't Vote
ART DIRECTOR *Marc Galucci*
CREATIVE DIRECTOR *Michael Sheehan*
COPYWRITER *Michael Sheehan*
ILLUSTRATORS *Kent Barton, Leslie Bistrowitz*
AGENCY *Clarke Goward*
CLIENT *Abigail Adams Historical Society*

She married a President.
She gave birth to a President.
Pity she couldn't vote for one.

John Adams
2nd U.S. President

John Quincy Adams
6th U.S. President

Abigail Smith Adams was, most certainly, one of America's more eminent women. In 1764, she wed John Adams, the second president of the United States. In 1767, she gave birth to John Quincy Adams, the sixth President of the United States. What's even more remarkable about her life is that she was, like every other American woman of the time, forbidden by law to vote for either of them. While her voice was silenced at the polls, her influence on both domestic and international matters was, in no way, subdued. To her husband and son, she was a valued counselor. Her letters touched on any number of timeless issues, including the poor financial state of the nation, the equality of women, and even the injustice of slavery. In one letter to her husband, she questioned the "passion of Liberty" among Virginians since they "have been accustomed to deprive their fellow Creatures of theirs." Her opinions on racial and sexual discrimination were, for the time, radical. Today, they are law. For a closer look at her life and times, visit the Abigail Adams Birthplace at North and Norton Streets in Weymouth. And pay tribute to America's most influential daughter. Not to mention wife and mother.

Abigail Adams Historical Society

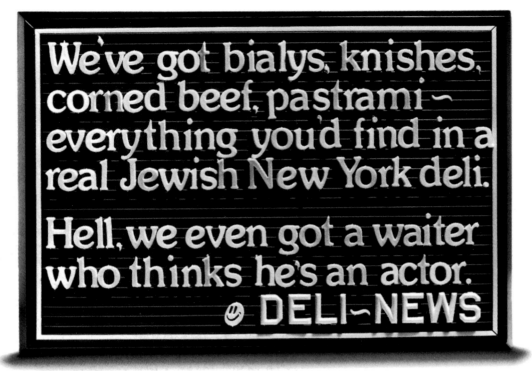

Two locations in Dallas: 15775 Hillcrest (392-3354) and 500 The Crescent Court (922-3354)

Distinctive Merit/National

LESS THAN A FULL PAGE
Waiter
ART DIRECTOR *Grant Richards*
CREATIVE DIRECTOR *Grant Richards*
COPYWRITER *Vinnie Chieco*
PRODUCER *Rebecca Brady*
AGENCY *The Richards Group*
CLIENT *Deli-News*

ANNCR.: *And now the story of Rapunzel and Her Golden Beer, as told by a paid spokesman for Rainier.*

MAN: *OK so once upon a time in Seattle there was this really big-haired Chi Omega Kega or Kappa Krappa Flappa or Ate-a Plate-a Ziti, anyway, some bowhead named Nancy Rapunzel III who supplied all the sorority parties with second-rate funk bands and this golden beer called Rainier, made with Yakima Valley hops and pure Cascade Mountain water from right here in the Northwest. So one night while Rapunzel was polishing her pearls, these really witchy girls from Delta Felta Shmelta kidnap her and the beer and lock 'em up in the Space Needle. So while Nancy's up in the tower crying "Why me, why me" the jealous Delta Feltas are throwing a party with some wimpy, trucked-in beer from St. Louis and even though the band was fresh the beer wasn't, so everyone from Alpha to Zeta heads over to the Space Needle where this guy named Moose screams "Rapunzel, Rapunzel, let down your beer." So Rapunzel undoes her big velvet bow, ties a case of Rainier to her long bleach-blonde hair and lowers it down to the thirsty crowd. So everybody's cheering and Rapunzel's feeling really good about herself until some Beta Theta Geeka yells out that 20 feet of her dark roots are showing. The end.*

ANNCR.: *Rainier. The beer from here. Rainier Brewing Company, Seattle, Washington.*

Merit/National

OUTDOOR, SINGLE
Sign from God
ART DIRECTOR *Mike Gustafson*
COPYWRITER *Eric Sorensen*
AGENCY *Chuck Ruhr Advertising*
CLIENT *St. Philip the Deacon*

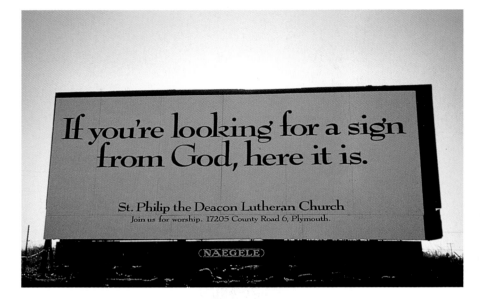

Merit/International

OUTDOOR, SINGLE
Pathfinder—Swiss Army
ART DIRECTOR *Carl van Wijk*
CREATIVE DIRECTORS *Carl van Wijk, Mark D'Arcy*
DESIGNER *Carl van Wijk*
COPYWRITER *Mark D'Arcy*
PHOTOGRAPHER *Chriss Lewis*
RETOUCHING *Grame Smallfield*
AGENCY *D'Arcy Masius Benton & Bowles,*
New Zealand
CLIENT *Nissan*

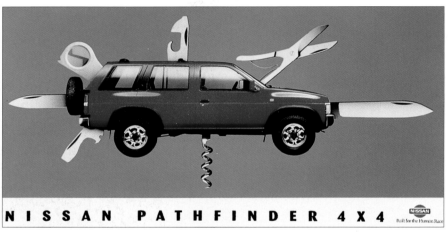

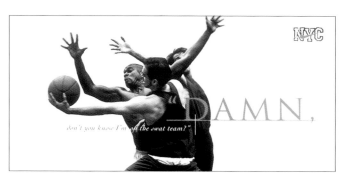

Merit/National

OUTDOOR, CAMPAIGN
Nike NYC "Trash Talk" 2nd series
ART DIRECTOR *John C. Jay*
CREATIVE DIRECTORS *Dan Wieden, Jamie Barrett,*
Jim Riswold
DESIGNER *Pao*
COPYWRITER *Jimmy Smith*
PHOTOGRAPHER *John Huet*
AGENCY *Wieden & Kennedy*
CLIENT *Nike*

Merit/National

OUTDOOR, CAMPAIGN
Nike NYC "Trash Talk" 1st series
ART DIRECTOR *John C. Jay*
CREATIVE DIRECTORS *Dan Wieden, Jamie Barrett,
Jim Riswold*
DESIGNER *Pao*
COPYWRITER *Jimmy Smith*
PHOTOGRAPHER *John Huet*
AGENCY *Wieden & Kennedy*
CLIENT *Nike*

Merit/International

TRANSIT, SINGLE
Loose Fit Dog
ART DIRECTOR *John Iredale*
CREATIVE DIRECTOR *Trevor Purvis*
COPYWRITERS *Jon Iredale, Matt McGrath*
ILLUSTRATOR *Jon Iredale*
AGENCY *McCann-Erickson, Sydney*
CLIENT *Levi Strauss Aust Pty Ltd*

Merit/National

TRANSIT, CAMPAIGN
Nike NYC "Graffiti" Wild Posting
ART DIRECTOR *John C. Jay*
CREATIVE DIRECTOR *John C. Jay*
DESIGNER *Chris Shipman*
PHOTOGRAPHER *Stanley Bach*
ILLUSTRATOR *Petra Langhammer*
AGENCY *Wieden & Kennedy*
CLIENT *Nike*

Merit/National

TRANSIT, CAMPAIGN
Steak, Commuter, Flyswatter
ART DIRECTORS *Tony Angotti, Max Jerome*
CREATIVE DIRECTORS *Tony Angotti, Dion Hughes*
COPYWRITERS *Dion Hughes, Steve Biegel*
PHOTOGRAPHERS *Jeff Divine, Jerry Cailor*
CLIENT *Molson Breweries USA, Inc.*

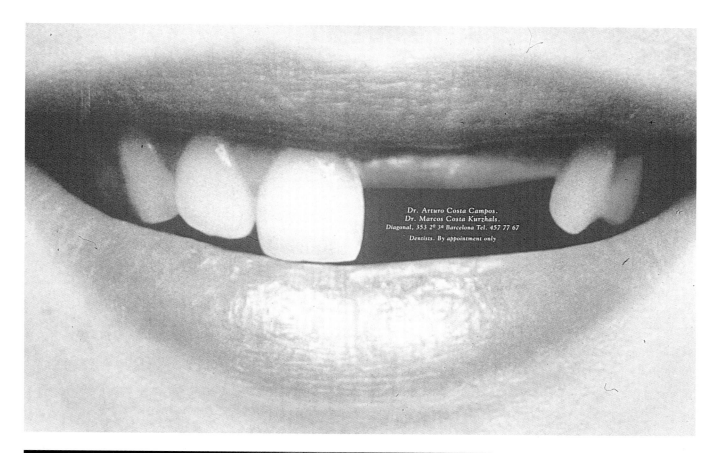

Dr. Arturo Costa Campos.
Dr. Marcos Costa Kurzhals.
Diagonal, 353 2ª 3ª Barcelona Tel. 457 77 67

Dentists. By appointment only

It would be unfair to suggest that all of the guys who wear Everlast crush beer cans on their foreheads.
But it is safe to assume you won't overhear them discussing the merits of a 1984 French Cabernet Sauvignon.

Merit/National

GENERAL, SINGLE
Earth General Diaper Poster
ART DIRECTOR *Debbie Klonk*
DESIGNER *Debbie Klonk*
COPYWRITER *Debbie Klonk*
AGENCY *Corn Fed Advertising*
CLIENT *Earth General*

Merit/National

GENERAL, SINGLE
Imagine Surviving Sexual Assault
ART DIRECTOR *Cliff Sorah*
CREATIVE DIRECTOR *Mike Hughes*
COPYWRITER *Joe Alexander*
PHOTOGRAPHERS *Martin Adler, Frank Fournier*
PRODUCER *Tom Maher*
AGENCY *The Martin Agency*
CLIENT *American Red Cross*

Merit/International

GENERAL, SINGLE
GAM, Graphic Arts Message, '94
ART DIRECTOR *Katsumi Asaba*
CREATIVE DIRECTOR *Naomi Enami*
DESIGNER *Daikoku Hisaya, Propeller Art Works Co., Ltd.*
PHOTOGRAPHER *Hajime Sawatari*
CLIENT *Too Corporation*

Merit/International

GENERAL, SINGLE
Diva
ART DIRECTOR *Katsumi Asaba*
DESIGNER *Keiko Mineishi*
PHOTOGRAPHER *Naruyasu Nabeshima*
CLIENT *Gaga Communications Inc.*

Merit/International

GENERAL, SINGLE
The 13th ISHII Award Typeface Contest Call for Entry
ART DIRECTOR *Katsumi Asaba*
DESIGNER *Keiko Mineishi*
COPYWRITER *Takako Terunuma*
ARTWORK *Hiroshi Tomura*
CLIENT *Shaken Co., Ltd.*

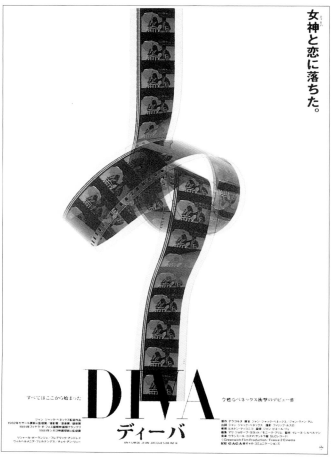

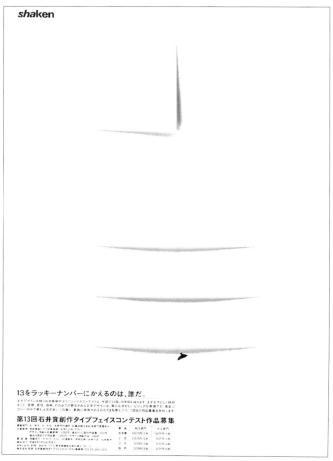

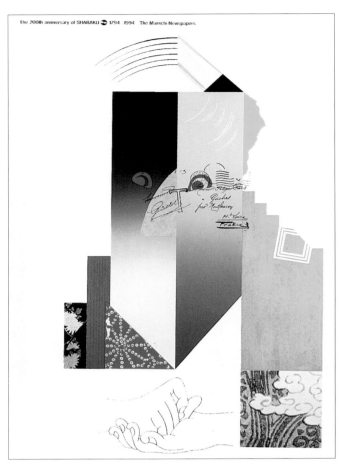

Merit/International

GENERAL, SINGLE
Basho Graphic Images
ART DIRECTOR *Masakazu Tanabe*
DESIGNER *Masakazu Tanabe*
ILLUSTRATORS *Masakazu Tanabe, Masahiko Hirano*
AGENCY *Media Co., Ltd.*
CLIENT *Chubu Creators Club*

Merit/International

GENERAL, SINGLE
The 200th Anniversary of Sharaku
ART DIRECTOR *Masakazu Tanabe*
DESIGNER *Masakazu Tanabe*
ILLUSTRATOR *Masakazu Tanabe*
AGENCY *Media Co., Ltd.*
CLIENT *The Mainichi Newspapers*

Merit/National

GENERAL, SINGLE
Poor Ratings
ART DIRECTOR *Grant Richards*
CREATIVE DIRECTORS *Todd Tilford, Grant Richards*
COPYWRITER *Todd Tilford*
PHOTOGRAPHER *Robb Debenport*
AGENCY *The Richards Group*
CLIENT *Tabu Lingerie*

Merit/International

GENERAL, SINGLE
Dictionary
ART DIRECTOR *Kins Lee*
DESIGNER *Kins Lee*
COPYWRITER *Janet Lee*
PHOTOGRAPHER *Stills Studio*
ILLUSTRATORS *Hau Theng Hui, Patrick Fong*
AGENCY *Spider Malaysia*
CLIENT *Cadbury Confectionary (M) SDN BHD*

Merit/International

GENERAL, SINGLE
Quality and Humanity
ART DIRECTOR *Kan Akita*
DESIGNERS *Kan Akita, Masayoshi Kodaira*
COPYWRITER *Shinzo Higurashi*
CLIENT *TOTO Ltd.*

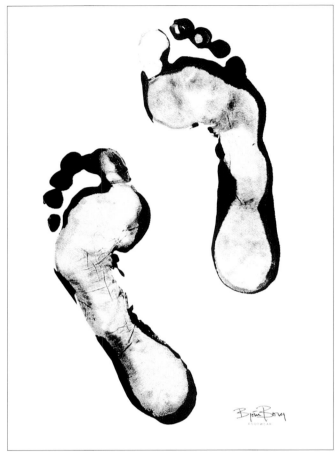

Merit/International

GENERAL, SINGLE
I Prefer Being Here to in the Sea
ART DIRECTOR *Masaharu Higashizawa*
CREATIVE DIRECTORS *Katsunori Tsuyama, Shuji Muya*
DESIGNERS *Shinji Kita, Takeshi Ishikawa,*
Yuko Onishi
COPYWRITER *Keisuke Yamashita*
PHOTOGRAPHER *Kanmei Matsumoto*
AGENCY *Daiko Advertising, Inc.*
CLIENT *Matsushita Electric Industrial Co.*

Merit/International

GENERAL, SINGLE
Bjorn Borg Footwear
ART DIRECTOR *Pelle Korberg*
CREATIVE DIRECTOR *Pelle Korberg*
COPYWRITER *Johan Brink*
PHOTOGRAPHER *Henrik Halvarsson*
AGENCY *Korberg & Co. Annonsbyra*
CLIENT *Scandinavian Footwear*

Merit/International

GENERAL, SINGLE
The 200th Anniversary of Sharaku
ART DIRECTOR *Masato Ohki*
DESIGNER *Masato Ohki*
PHOTOGRAPHER *Masato Ohki*
SCULPTOR *Masato Ohki*
CLIENT *The Mainichi Newspapers*

Merit/International

GENERAL, SINGLE
Eating This
ART DIRECTOR *Bradley Wood*
CREATIVE DIRECTOR *Peter McHugh*
DESIGNERS *Bob Rickert, Bradley Wood*
COPYWRITER *Bob Rickert*
PHOTOGRAPHER *Joe Jacobs*
AGENCY *Chiat/Day Inc. Advertising*
CLIENT *Ontario Ministry of Transportation*

Merit/National

GENERAL, CAMPAIGN
What You Can Do with Frozen Beef Trayliner
ART DIRECTOR *Steve Sandstrom*
CREATIVE DIRECTOR *Steve Sandoz*
DESIGNER *Steve Sandstrom*
COPYWRITER *Steve Sandoz*
ILLUSTRATOR *Eric Larsen*
AGENCIES *Sandstrom Design, Artsy Fartsy Productions*
CLIENT *Burgerville USA*

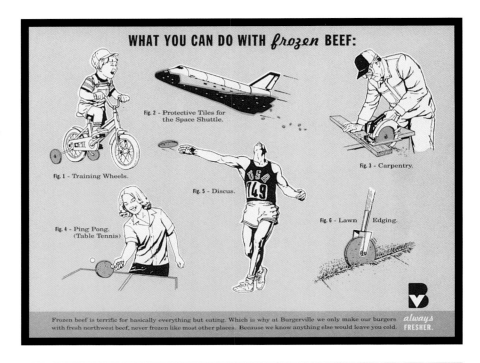

Merit/National

GENERAL, CAMPAIGN
Burger Hockey Trayliner
ART DIRECTOR *Steve Sandstrom*
CREATIVE DIRECTOR *Steve Sandoz*
DESIGNER *Steve Sandstrom*
COPYWRITER *Steve Sandoz*
AGENCIES *Sandstrom Design, Artsy Fartsy Productions*
CLIENT *Burgerville USA*

Merit/International

GENERAL, CAMPAIGN
HIT
ART DIRECTORS *Zempaku Suzuki, Jun Ueno*
DESIGNERS *Zempaku Suzuki, Masahiro Naito*
COPYWRITER *Mariko Hayashi*
ILLUSTRATOR *Hanna-Barbera*
AGENCY *Dentsu, Inc.*
STUDIO *B-BI Studio Inc.*
CLIENT *The Toyo Trust & Banking Co., Ltd.*

Merit/International

GENERAL, CAMPAIGN
King Printing
ART DIRECTOR *Koji Mizutani*
CREATIVE DIRECTOR *Koji Mizutani*
DESIGNER *Hiroshi Ohmizo*
ILLUSTRATOR *Hiroshi Ohmizo*
AGENCY *Mizutani Studio*
STUDIO *Mizutani Studio*
CLIENT *King Printing Co., Ltd.*

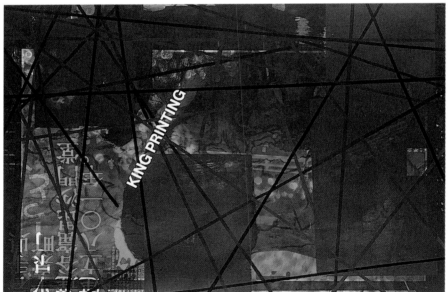

Merit/International

GENERAL, CAMPAIGN
Push — In Order to Make Life Fun
ART DIRECTOR *Koichi Sawada*
CREATIVE DIRECTOR *Hiroshi Sasaki*
DESIGNERS *Yuji Tokuda, Kazuaki Aikawa,*
Takahiro Kurashima
COPYWRITERS *Naoto Ohdate, Tetsuya Watanabe*
PHOTOGRAPHER *Eiichiro Sakata*
ILLUSTRATOR *Koichi Sawada*
ART *Yasuhide Kobayashi*
AGENCY *Dentsu, Inc.*
STUDIO *Dentsu Cotec & Common Design*
CLIENT *Fuji Television Network*

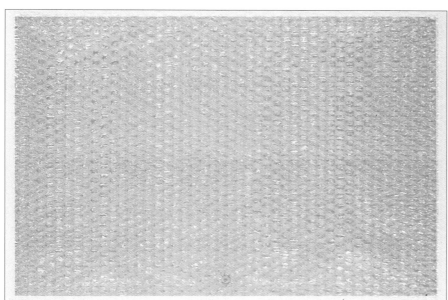

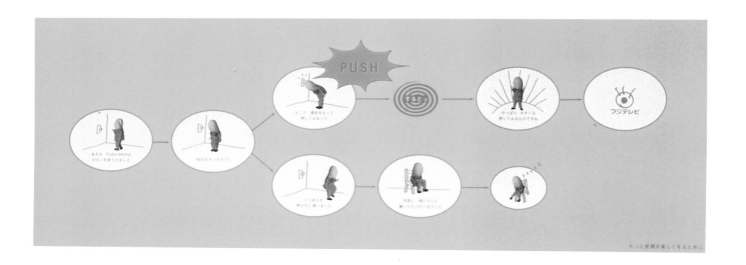

Merit/International

GENERAL, CAMPAIGN
A Light Bulb, A Disciple, The Queen's Husband
ART DIRECTOR *Carl van Wijk*
CREATIVE DIRECTOR *Raj Marwah*
DESIGNER *Carl van Wijk*
COPYWRITER *Mark D'Arcy*
PRODUCER *John Hutchinson*
AGENCY *D'Arcy Masius Benton & Bowles,*
New Zealand
CLIENT *Phillips Fox*

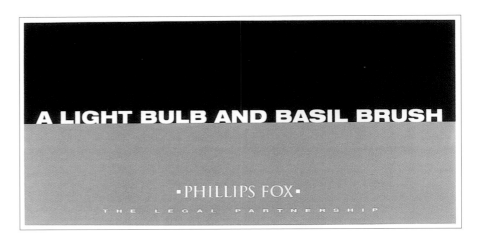

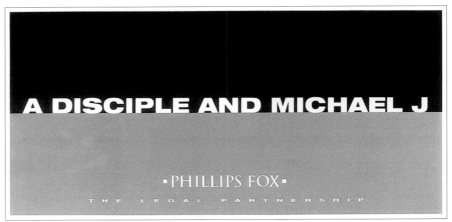

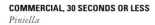

Merit/National

COMMERCIAL, 30 SECONDS OR LESS
Buddy
ART DIRECTOR *Jerry Gentile*
CREATIVE DIRECTOR *Steve Rabosky*
COPYWRITER *Scott Vincent*
PRODUCERS *Michelle Burke, Jeff Gorman*
AGENCY *Chiat/Day Inc. Advertising*
CLIENT *Sunkist California Pistachios*

Merit/National

COMMERCIAL, 30 SECONDS OR LESS
Piniella
ART DIRECTOR *Kristy Willson*
CREATIVE DIRECTOR *Jim Walker*
COPYWRITERS *John Schofield, Jim Copacino*
PRODUCER *Michelle Woodruff*
AGENCY *McCann-Erickson Seattle*
CLIENT *Mariners Baseball*

Merit/National

COMMERCIAL, 30 SECONDS OR LESS
Buhner
ART DIRECTOR *Kristy Willson*
CREATIVE DIRECTOR *Jim Walker*
COPYWRITERS *John Schofield, Jim Copacino*
PRODUCER *Michelle Woodruff*
AGENCY *McCann-Erickson Seattle*
CLIENT *Mariners Baseball*

Merit/National

COMMERCIAL, 30 SECONDS OR LESS
Universal Excuses
ART DIRECTOR *Mark Oakley*
CREATIVE DIRECTORS *Todd Seisser, Jay Taub*
COPYWRITER *David Bernstein*
PRODUCER *Susan Shipman*
DIRECTOR *Jeff Stark*
AGENCY *Ammirati & Puris, Lintas*
CLIENT *United Parcel Service*

Merit/National

COMMERCIAL, 30 SECONDS OR LESS
Choir
ART DIRECTOR *Rick Rabe*
CREATIVE DIRECTOR *Parry Merkley*
COPYWRITER *David Leite*
PRODUCER *Will McDonald*
DIRECTOR *Graham Henman*
AGENCY *Merkley Newman Harty, Inc.*
CLIENT *Casio, Inc.*

Merit/National

COMMERCIAL, 30 SECONDS OR LESS
You'll Love the Way It Wears—Rug
ART DIRECTOR *Bob Ranew*
COPYWRITER *Liz Paradise*
AGENCY *McKinney and Silver*
CLIENT *Karastan-Bigelow*

Merit/National

COMMERCIAL, 30 SECONDS OR LESS
It's All Fuel
ART DIRECTOR *Jeanne Byers*
CREATIVE DIRECTOR *Rochelle Klein*
COPYWRITER *Rochelle Klein*
PRODUCER *Pam Ferman*
DIRECTOR *Osbert Parker*
MUSIC *Bruce Wooley*
AGENCY *Angotti, Thomas, Hedge, Inc.*
CLIENT *Sun Company, Inc.*

Merit/National

COMMERCIAL, 30 SECONDS OR LESS
Chihuahua
ART DIRECTOR *Kent Johnson*
CREATIVE DIRECTORS *Glenn Dady, Mike Malone*
COPYWRITERS *David Coats, Kevin Sutton*
PRODUCER *Carol Leftwich*
DIRECTOR *Robert Hannant*
AGENCY *The Richards Group*
CLIENT *EyeMasters*

Merit/National

COMMERCIAL, 30 SECONDS OR LESS
The State "More Miserable Crap"
ART DIRECTOR *Kenan Moran*
CREATIVE DIRECTOR *Angie Li*
PRODUCER *Kenan Moran*
DIRECTOR *Kenan Moran*
AGENCY *MTV Networks*
CLIENT *MTV*

Merit/National

COMMERCIAL, 30 SECONDS OR LESS
Dumplings
ART DIRECTOR *Doug Hill*
CREATIVE DIRECTOR *Mike Drazen*
COPYWRITER *Kelly Simmons*
PRODUCER *Pat Cannon*
DIRECTOR *Mark Tiedemann*
MUSIC *Tomandandy*
AGENCY *Earle Palmer Brown, Philadelphia*
STUDIO *Crossroads Films*
CLIENT *The Philadelphia Inquirer*

Merit/National

COMMERCIAL, 30 SECONDS OR LESS
Dreyer's Cop
ART DIRECTOR *Joey LaCascia*
CREATIVE DIRECTORS *Brian O'Neil, Paul Carek*
PHOTOGRAPHER *D. P. Kirk Bachman*
PRODUCERS *Michael King, Debra Trotz*
DIRECTOR *Brenton Thomas*
MUSIC *Ad Music, Los Angeles*
AGENCY *Goldberg, Moser, O'Neil*
CLIENT *Dreyer's Grand Ice Cream*

Merit/International

COMMERCIAL, 30 SECONDS OR LESS
Spur
ART DIRECTOR *Jordi Almuni*
CREATIVE DIRECTORS *Paco Segarra,*
Manolo Portabella
COPYWRITER *Juan Finger*
DIRECTOR *João Daniel Thikomiroff*
MUSIC *Red Back*
AGENCY *Vinizius/Young & Rubicam*
CLIENT *Textil Zedesa*

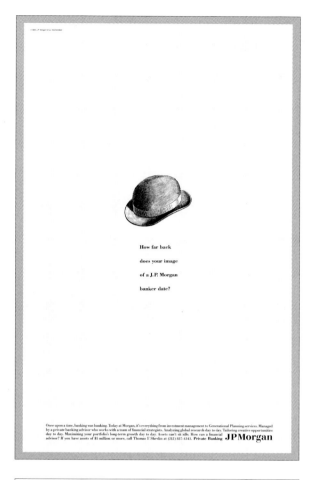

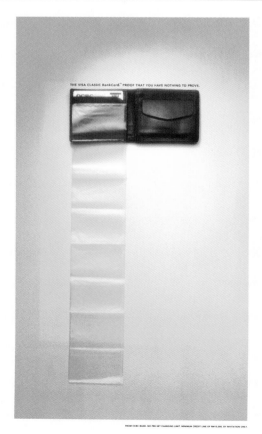

Merit/National

FULL PAGE OR SPREAD
Derby
ART DIRECTOR *Gary Goldsmith*
CREATIVE DIRECTOR *Gary Goldsmith*
COPYWRITER *Dean Hacohen*
ILLUSTRATOR *Christopher Wormell*
AGENCY *Goldsmith/Jeffrey*
CLIENT *J. P. Morgan Private Banking*

Merit/International

FULL PAGE OR SPREAD
Corn Kernel
ART DIRECTOR *Terry Iles*
CREATIVE DIRECTOR *Michael Fromowitz*
COPYWRITER *John Kewley*
ILLUSTRATOR *Rod Grigor*
AGENCY *McCann-Erickson/Toronto*
STUDIO *Lakefront Studio*
CLIENT *Nabisco Brands Ltd (Del Monte)*

Merit/International

FULL PAGE OR SPREAD
Wallet
ART DIRECTOR *Steven Ang*
CREATIVE DIRECTOR *Rick Lane*
COPYWRITERS *Rick Lane, Steven Ang*
PHOTOGRAPHER *Hock of Studio Pashe*
AGENCY *Dentsu, Young & Rubicam*
CLIENT *Overseas Chinese Banking Corporation*

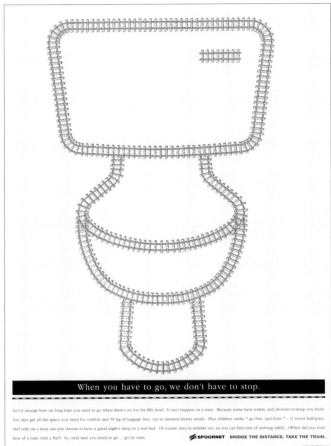

Merit/International

FULL PAGE OR SPREAD
Tomato Sprig
ART DIRECTOR *Terry Iles*
CREATIVE DIRECTOR *Michael Fromowitz*
COPYWRITER *John Kewley*
ILLUSTRATOR *Rod Grigor*
AGENCY *McCann-Erickson/Toronto*
STUDIO *Lakefront Studio*
CLIENT *Nabisco Brands Ltd (Del Monte)*

Merit/International

FULL PAGE OR SPREAD
When You Have to Go
ART DIRECTOR *Mike Rossi*
CREATIVE DIRECTORS *Gaby Bush, Graham de Lacy*
COPYWRITER *Athalie Russell*
ILLUSTRATOR *Mike Rossi*
AGENCY *Lindsay Smithers-FCB*
CLIENT *Spoornet*

Merit/International

FULL PAGE OR SPREAD
Raffles Hotel Opens a Singles Bar
ART DIRECTOR *Grover Tham*
CREATIVE DIRECTOR *Tim Evill*
COPYWRITERS *Jim Aitchison, Kash Sree,*
Tham Khai Meng
AGENCY *Batey Ads Singapore*
CLIENT *Raffles Hotel, Singapore*

A micro ad. What else would you expect from a small brewery in Oregon?
Try Weinhard's Boar's Head Red Lager.

For a good look at our beer, see your bartender. Or your optometrist. *Try Henry Weinhard's Private Reserve.*

Henry Weinhard's Private Reserve is here. Unfortunately, right now, it's as hard to find as our ads.

Merit/International

CAMPAIGN
Remember Qatar, No More Yellow Cards
ART DIRECTOR *Hiroaki Shuto*
CREATIVE DIRECTOR *Shinsuke Kasahara*
DESIGNERS *Koji Yamada, Gen Ishii*
COPYWRITER *Tomomi Maeda*
PHOTOGRAPHER *Kazumi Kurigami*
AGENCY *Hakuhodo, Inc.*
CLIENT *SONY Creative Products Inc.*

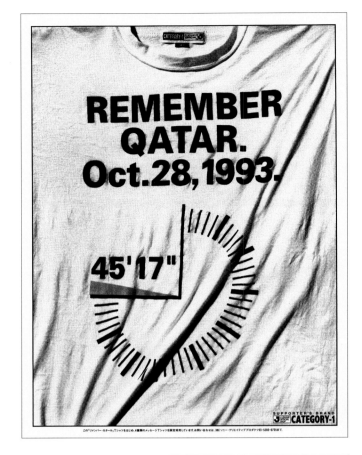

Merit/International

FULL PAGE OR SPREAD
Just One of the Lives
ART DIRECTOR *Lye Kok Hong*
CREATIVE DIRECTORS *Jim Aitchison, Tim Evill*
COPYWRITERS *Daniel Lim, Jim Aitchison, Tim Evill*
PHOTOGRAPHY *Procolor*
AGENCY *Batey Ads Singapore*
CLIENT *Mercedes-Benz Asia*

Merit/International

FULL PAGE OR SPREAD
Better Buy a Honda Motorcycle
ART DIRECTOR *Carlos Garcia*
CREATIVE DIRECTOR *Nizao Guanaes*
COPYWRITER *Carlos Domingos*
PHOTOGRAPHY *Agencia Estado*
PRODUCER *Anelito Nobrega*
AGENCY *DM9 Publicidade*
CLIENT *Moto Honda da Amazonia*

Merit/National

CAMPAIGN
Aromas, Ingredients, Beauty
ART DIRECTOR *Amy Watt*
CREATIVE DIRECTORS *Edward Boches, Amy Watt*
COPYWRITER *Edward Boches*
AGENCY *Mullen*
CLIENT *Aveda Corporation*

Truly natural aromas are found in
flowers, leaves, roots and barks.

Not glued to the pages of this magazine.

The ingredients in our products aren't purchased,
procured or acquired. They're borrowed.

From the earth.

Most cosmetic companies go to New York,
Paris and Milan to learn about beauty.

We go to the Rain Forest.

The game of golf was created in Scotland in 1744. But that doesn't mean the meal afterwards should taste that way.

THOUGHT OF 108 HOLES OF GOLF WHET YOUR APPETITE? THEN COME ENJOY UNLIMITED GOLF ON FIVE COURSES. FLAT COURSES, ROLLING COURSES, LET'S [$166*] JUST SAY YOU'LL NEVER BE BORED. OUR "GOLF HOLIDAY" ALSO INCLUDES BREAKFAST AND DINNER IN YOUR CHOICE OF RESTAURANTS, INCLUD- ING THE MEMORABLE EL BIZCOCHO (TOP-RATED IN SAN DIEGO). ALL INCLUDED FOR ONE PRICE. CALL US AT 1-800-542-6096.

IS THERE SOME OBSCURE GOLF RULE SOMEWHERE THAT SAYS GREAT GOLF AND GREAT FOOD MUST BE MUTUALLY EXCLUSIVE? IF SO, WE CHALLENGE IT EVERY DAY AT THE RANCHO BERNARDO INN. AND SPEAK- ING OF CHALLENGES, DOES THE

RANCHO BERNARDO INN
The way the world is supposed to be.

WE'VE ALWAYS BEEN. UNPRETENTIOUS AND GENUINE. [$166*] SO WHY NOT TAKE A BREAK AND JOIN US? YOU CAN PLAY UNLIMITED GOLF ON FIVE COURSES, 108 HOLES IN ALL. THERE'S TENNIS AND A SPA. BREAKFAST AND DINNER

The holidays are a perfect time to spend with loved ones. (Do a masseuse and a room service waiter qualify as loved ones?)

IN THE MIDDLE OF ALL THE HOLIDAY RUSH-RUSH-RUSH, DON'T FORGET TO STOP, RELAX AND ENJOY. WE'RE ALL DRESSED UP FOR THE OCCASION. THE LIGHTS ARE IN THE TREES — AND THERE ARE A LOT OF TREES. WINE GLASSES ARE SPARKLING. THE FIREPLACE IS WARMED UP. AND SO ARE THE CAROLERS. BUT WE'RE STILL THE SAME PLACE ARE INCLUDED EACH DAY—AND IT WILL BE A DINNER YOU WISH WOULD NEVER END. ISN'T THIS HOW TRADITIONS GET STARTED? 1-800-542-6096.

RANCHO BERNARDO INN
The way the world is supposed to be

Most golf pros advise you to spend plenty of time warming up before a round. So, how does 72 degrees sound?

LIKE TOMORROW (SAME AS TODAY). THE RANCHO BERNARDO INN, NORTH OF SAN DIEGO. [$166*] THAW OUT YOUR SWING ON FIVE DIFFERENT COURSES, 108 HOLES IN ALL. THERE'S A HEALTH SPA AND TENNIS, AS YOU'D EXPECT. BUT, AS YOU WOULDN'T EXPECT, BREAKFAST AND DINNER ARE INCLUDED EACH DAY. AND THE FOOD HAS BEEN RATED AMONG THE BEST IN ALL OF

IF THE THOUGHT OF A FRESHLY MOWED FAIRWAY SEEMS MORE APPEALING THAN FRESHLY PLOWED SNOW, ESCAPE TO A PLACE WHERE THE MOOD IS WARM, THE PEOPLE ARE WARMER AND YOU DON'T HAVE TO WASTE ANY TIME WONDERING WHAT THE WEATHER IS GOING TO BE SAN DIEGO. (GREAT GOLF AND GREAT FOOD IN ONE LOCATION? YES, THIS IS PARADISE.) 1-800-542-6096.

RANCHO BERNARDO INN
The way the world is supposed to be

Merit/National

CAMPAIGN
RBI Magazine Campaign: The Game of Golf, Loved Ones, Warming Up
ART DIRECTOR *John Vitro*
CREATIVE DIRECTION *VITROROBERTSON*
COPYWRITER *John Robertson*
ILLUSTRATOR *Tracy Sabin*
AGENCY *VITROROBERTSON*
CLIENT *JC Resorts*

When you consider the strength
of Minnesota's forests, maybe the
Land of 10,000 Lakes should be called
the Land of 10,000,000,000 Trees.

That might be a little too long to fit on our license plates, but it pretty much sums up Minnesota's forests.

As you can imagine, ten billion trees in a state of our size make for some vast forest lands. In fact, forests cover a full third of our state. They support 24 different kinds of trees and are home to countless species of wildlife.

Of course, it's not just the size of our forests that's important. It's also their health and vitality. (Research indicates that a managed forest is more resistant to diseases and catastrophic fires.) As it is, 28 trees die of natural causes for every one tree harvested.

Yet every year thirty-one new trees spring up in their places.

Ultimately that leads not only to more trees, but also healthier trees in a state where our forests are as much a part of our quality of life as, well...our lakes.

According to a recent environmental study, planned timber harvesting will not negatively impact sedimentation, streamflow patterns, or fish populations.

M i n n e s o t a   F o r e s t   I n d u s t r i e s

© 1994 Minnesota Forest Industries

Statistics show that if you
grow up in Minnesota you'll be stronger,
healthier and better looking.
(Particularly if you're a tree.)

It's only natural that a state's forests should reflect the values of the people who take care of them.

Which may be why Minnesota forests are in good shape.

This according to the most comprehensive environmental impact study ever conducted on timber harvesting.

Forests cover a third of our state. Recent U.S. Forest Service inventories show 20 million trees have diameters greater than 19 inches. That's six million more large trees than existed just fifteen years ago.

The tightrope walk between our economic growth and forest management is difficult. But our state does it well—better, in fact, than other states.

We can all share the credit. Conservation interests, private landowners, governmental bodies and our forest industries are all working together to make a difference.

After all, isn't that the Minnesota way?

Since 1980, more than 243 million trees have been planted in Minnesota by public and private groups.

M i n n e s o t a   F o r e s t   I n d u s t r i e s

© 1994 Minnesota Forest Industries

Merit/National

CAMPAIGN
Forest Campaign
ART DIRECTOR *Bill Winchester*
CREATIVE DIRECTOR *Bill Winchester*
COPYWRITER *Tom Evans*
PHOTOGRAPHER *Craig Perman*
AGENCY *Colle & McVoy Marketing Communications*
CLIENT *Minnesota Forest Industries*

Ironically, the state that's
home to the world's most famous
logger has some of the best
forests in the country.

You wouldn't think a society that honored a larger-than-life mythical figure like Paul Bunyan would have any forests left to speak of.

Yet the truth is, according to the largest environmental impact study ever to assess timber harvesting anywhere in the world, Minnesota's forests are in good shape.

And along with the state and local governments, forest industries themselves have done much to manage our forests effectively.

The result? Over 10 billion trees are growing in Minnesota today. Statewide, the latest U.S. Forest Service Inventory shows tree volume has increased 25% since 1977. And there will be more trees in the 1990s than in any decade since official records have been kept.

We're proud of how forestry has kept evolving for the better.

We think Minnesota should be, too.

Every year in Minnesota, more trees grow than are harvested. In fact, only 1% of our 16.6 million acres of woodlands is annually harvested.

M i n n e s o t a   F o r e s t   I n d u s t r i e s

© 1994 Minnesota Forest Industries

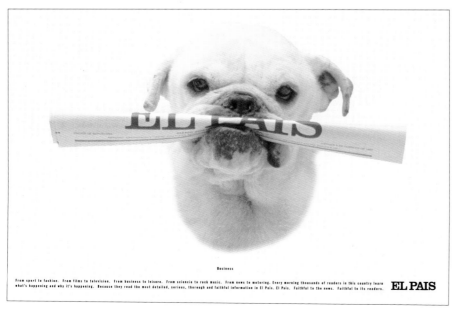

Merit/International

CAMPAIGN
Faithful
ART DIRECTOR *Ramón Roda*
CREATIVE DIRECTORS *Xavi García, Angel Sanchez*
COPYWRITERS *Xavi García, Angel Sanchez*
PHOTOGRAPHER *David Levin*
AGENCY *Casadevall Pedreño & PRG*
CLIENT *Diario el País, S.A.*

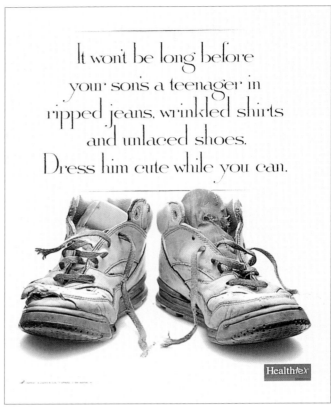

Merit/National

LESS THAN A FULL PAGE
Renoir
ART DIRECTOR *Jamie Mahoney*
CREATIVE DIRECTOR *Mike Hughes*
COPYWRITER *Joe Alexander*
PHOTOGRAPHY *Dublin Productions*
PRODUCER *Kay Franz*
AGENCY *The Martin Agency*
CLIENT *Healthtex, Inc.*

Merit/National

LESS THAN A FULL PAGE
Teenager
ART DIRECTOR *Jamie Mahoney*
CREATIVE DIRECTOR *Mike Hughes*
COPYWRITER *Raymond McKinney*
PHOTOGRAPHY *Dublin Productions*
PRODUCER *Kay Franz*
AGENCY *The Martin Agency*
CLIENT *Healthtex, Inc.*

Merit/National

LESS THAN A FULL PAGE
Someone Feeds You
ART DIRECTOR *Jamie Mahoney*
CREATIVE DIRECTOR *Mike Hughes*
COPYWRITER *Joe Alexander*
PHOTOGRAPHY *Dublin Productions*
PRODUCER *Kay Franz*
AGENCY *The Martin Agency*
CLIENT *Healthtex, Inc.*

Merit/National

FULL PAGE OR SPREAD
Paris, Texas
ART DIRECTOR *Margaret McGovern*
CREATIVE DIRECTORS *Paul Silverman,*
Margaret McGovern
COPYWRITER *Paul Silverman*
PHOTOGRAPHER *John Holt Studio*
AGENCY *Mullen*
CLIENT *The Timberland Company*

Merit/National

FULL PAGE OR SPREAD
Laughing Bugs
ART DIRECTOR *Hal Tench*
CREATIVE DIRECTOR *Hal Tench*
COPYWRITER *Raymond McKinney*
ILLUSTRATOR *Hal Mayfordth*
PRODUCER *Karen Smith*
AGENCY *The Martin Agency*
CLIENT *FMC Corporation*

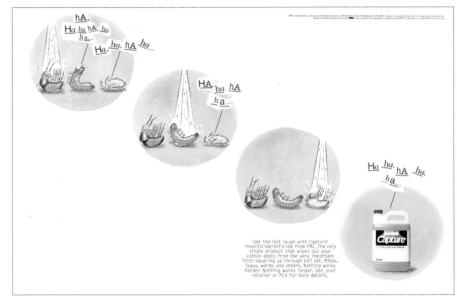

Merit/National

CAMPAIGN
Bats, Fireworks, Pterodactyl
ART DIRECTORS *Jim Mountjoy, Andy Azula*
CREATIVE DIRECTOR *Jim Mountjoy*
DESIGNER *Jim Mountjoy*
COPYWRITERS *Ed Jones, Bill Milkereit*
PHOTOGRAPHER *Jim Arndt*
AGENCY *Loeffler Ketchum Mountjoy*
CLIENT *Verbatim*

(left)
Merit/International

CAMPAIGN
EPSON: Prison, Tatouage, Dalmatien, Le Nu,
Parchemin
ART DIRECTOR *Robin de Lestrade*
CREATIVE DIRECTOR *Jean-Claude Jouis*
COPYWRITER *Olivier Altman*
PHOTOGRAPHER *Robin de Lestrade*
AGENCY *BDDP*
CLIENT *EPSON*

(facing page)
Merit/International

CAMPAIGN
Spots, 30 Seconds
ART DIRECTOR *Gary Marshall*
CREATIVE DIRECTORS *Paul Marshall, Gary Marshall*
DESIGNER *Gary Marshall*
COPYWRITER *Paul Marshall*
PHOTOGRAPHER *Dean Steadman*
AGENCY *Bean MC*
CLIENT *Laser Sales*

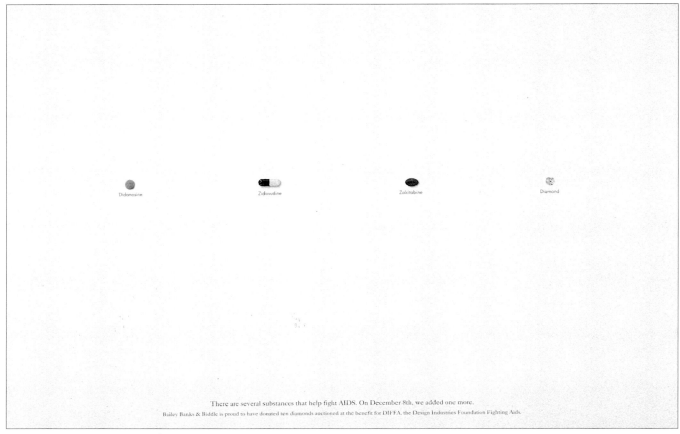

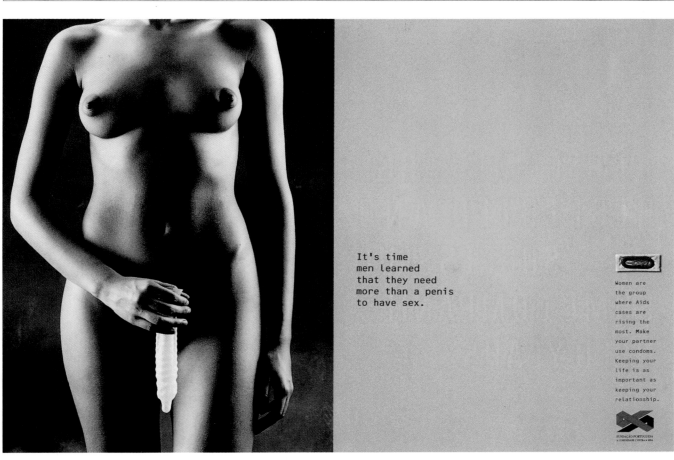

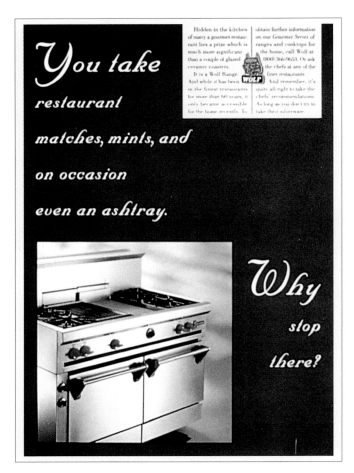

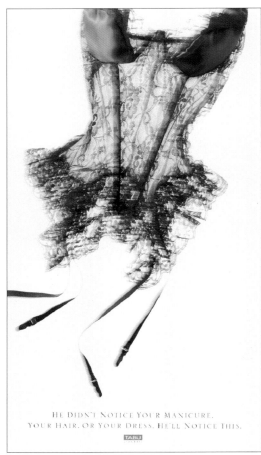

Merit/National

SINGLE
You Take
ART DIRECTOR *Michael Kadin*
COPYWRITERS *Renee Miller, David Stolberg*
PHOTOGRAPHER *Markku*
AGENCY *The Miller Group*
CLIENT *Wolf Range Co.*

Merit/National

SINGLE
Notice
ART DIRECTOR *Grant Richards*
CREATIVE DIRECTORS *Todd Tilford, Grant Richards*
COPYWRITER *Todd Tilford*
PHOTOGRAPHER *Robb Debenport*
PRODUCER *Gail Beckman*
AGENCY *The Richards Group*
STUDIO *Laser Tech Color*
CLIENT *Tabu Lingerie*

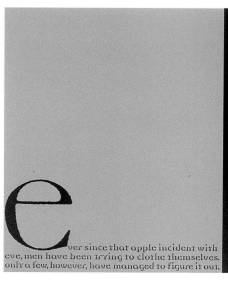

ever since that apple incident with eve, men have been trying to clothe themselves. only a few, however, have managed to figure it out.

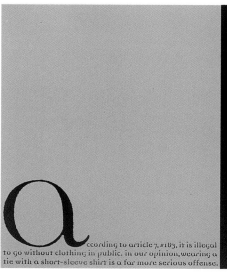

according to article 7, #183, it is illegal to go without clothing in public. in our opinion, wearing a tie with a short-sleeve shirt is a far more serious offense.

to attract a female, all a male grasshopper has to do is rub his legs together. man doesn't have it so easy.

Merit/National

CAMPAIGN
Apple Incident, Serious Offense, Grasshopper
ART DIRECTOR *Eric Tilford*
CREATIVE DIRECTOR *Todd Tilford*
COPYWRITER *Todd Tilford*
PHOTOGRAPHER *Richard Reens*
PRODUCER *Gail Beckman*
AGENCY *The Richards Group*
STUDIO *Laser Tech Color*
CLIENT *Lombardo Custom Apparel*

Merit/International

CAMPAIGN
Mandela Cup Cricket Package
ART DIRECTOR *Red Nail*
CREATIVE DIRECTOR *Red Nail*
DESIGNER *Red Nail*
COPYWRITER *Red Nail*
PHOTOGRAPHER *Michael Meyersfeld*
AGENCY *Red Nail*
STUDIO *Red Nail*
CLIENT *TV1*

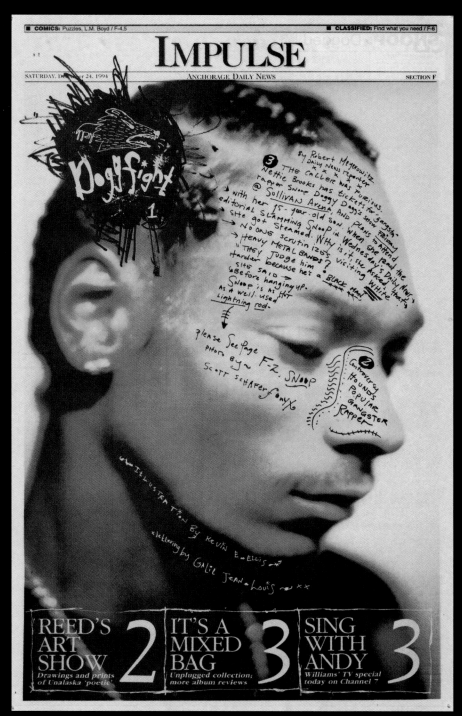

Gold Medalist/National

FULL PAGE OR SPREAD
Doggfight
ART DIRECTOR *Galie Jean-Louis*
CREATIVE DIRECTOR *Galie Jean-Louis*
DESIGNER *Galie Jean-Louis*
PHOTOGRAPHER *Scott Schafer*
ILLUSTRATOR *Kevin E. Ellis*
STUDIO *Galie Jean-Louis*
CLIENT *Anchorage Daily News*

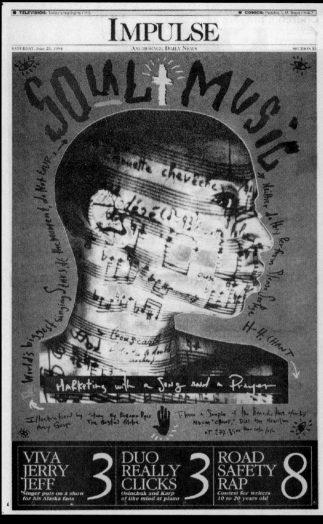

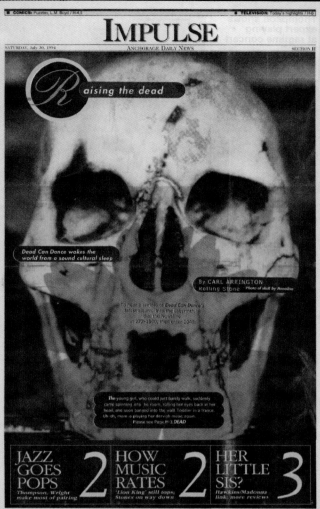

Silver Medalist/National

FULL PAGE OR SPREAD
Soul Music
ART DIRECTOR *Galie Jean-Louis*
CREATIVE DIRECTOR *Galie Jean-Louis*
DESIGNER *Galie Jean-Louis*
PHOTOGRAPHER *Amy Guip*
ILLUSTRATOR *Galie Jean-Louis*
STUDIO *Galie Jean-Louis*
CLIENT *Anchorage Daily News*

Silver Medalist/National

FULL PAGE OR SPREAD
Raising the Dead
ART DIRECTOR *Galie Jean-Louis*
CREATIVE DIRECTOR *Galie Jean-Louis*
DESIGNER *Galie Jean-Louis*
PHOTOGRAPHER *Annalisa*
STUDIO *Galie Jean-Louis*
CLIENT *Anchorage Daily News*

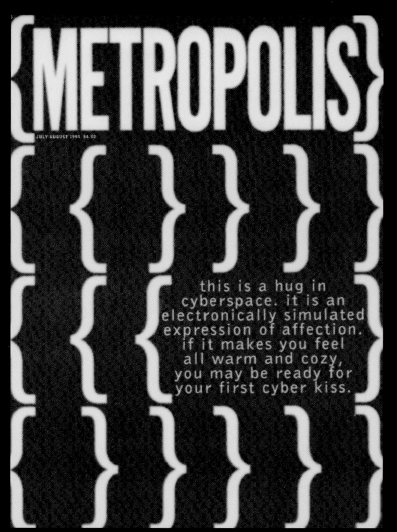

Silver Medalist/National

COVER
This Is a Hug in Cyberspace
ART DIRECTORS *Carl Lehmann-Haupt,*
Nancy Kruger Cohen
DESIGNERS *Carl Lehmann-Haupt,*
Nancy Kruger Cohen
EDITOR *Susan Szenasy*
COPYWRITER *Karrie Jacobs*
CLIENT *Metropolis*

Silver Medalist/National

FULL PAGE OR SPREAD
Man of the Year
CREATIVE DIRECTOR *Fred Woodward*
DESIGNER *Geraldine Hessler*
ILLUSTRATOR *David Cowles*
CLIENT *Rolling Stone*

ADDITIONAL AWARD

Distinctive Merit
ILLUSTRATION, EDITORIAL, FULL PAGE OR SPREAD

225

Gold Medalist/National

SPECIAL EFFECTS AND COMPUTER GRAPHICS, SINGLE
Frogs
ART DIRECTOR *Michael Smith*
CREATIVE DIRECTORS *Michael Hutchinson,*
Ric Anello
COPYWRITER *Dave Swaine*
ANIMATRONICS *Stan Winston Studio*
PRODUCER *Chan Hatcher*
DIRECTOR *Gore Verbinski*
MUSIC *Tom Woodard, Hummingbird*
AGENCY *D'Arcy Masius Benton & Bowles*
CLIENT *Anheuser-Busch/Budweiser*

ADDITIONAL AWARD

Silver Medalist
ADVERTISING, TELEVISION, COMMERCIAL,
30 SECONDS OR LESS

Silver Medalist/National

BOOKLET, FOLDER, OR BROCHURE, SERIES
The Edison Project Booklets
ART DIRECTORS *Stephen Doyle, Tom Kluepfel*
DESIGNERS *Rosemarie Turk, Gary Tooth,*
Mats Hakansson, Katrin Schmitt-Tegge
ILLUSTRATORS *Brian Cairns, Jessie Hartland,*
Allan Drummond, Jon Agee
PHOTOGRAPHER *Gentl & Hyers*
STUDIO *Drenttel Doyle Partners*
CLIENT *The Edison Project*

Named one of the top U.S. Companies to work for in *The 100 Best Companies to Work for in America*, Herman Miller has been a design leader for decades. (But is it fun to work there?) Under the leadership of creative director Stephen Frykholm (He's a real gas!), the team at Herman Miller has helped the company win awards like the AIGA Design Leadership and Fortune & American Center for Design Beacon Award. The NY Art Director's Club, CA, Graphis, ID, and AIGA Communication Graphics have also recognized Herman Miller's graphic design. (Some of these awards are really cool.) Herman Miller offers an attractive beginning designer's salary (not g___ but enough to pay the rent). Interested candidates ___ a BFA or MFA degree (and a lively imaginat___ ly by sending a maximum of twenty slides of re___ and a resume by june, 1994. Please include educa___ and work experience references. (Don't worry, young designers getting the job before you didn't have much either.) Send resumes to: Herman Miller Inc., Staffing department 0162, PO Box 302, Zeeland, Michigan 49464-0302. (Don't try to buck the system by sending your stuff directly to Steve. He'll lose it.) Include a self-addressed, stamped envelope for return of slides; please do not send actual portfolios. Selected candidates will be contacted by August, 1994 to arrange interviews. (We'll buy lunch and give you the real low-down.)

Silver Medalist/National

POSTER, OTHER THAN ADVERTISING, SINGLE
Herman Miller Design Position Poster
ART DIRECTOR *Yang Kim*
CREATIVE DIRECTOR *Yang Kim*
DESIGNER *Yang Kim*
COPYWRITER *Clark Malcolm*
ILLUSTRATOR *Yang Kim*
PRINTER *Etheridge Company*
CLIENT *Herman Miller Inc.*

Silver Medalist/National

POSTER, OTHER THAN ADVERTISING, SINGLE
Was/Saw
ART DIRECTOR *Stephen Doyle*
DESIGNER *Gary Tooth*
PHOTOGRAPHER *Davies & Starr*
STUDIO *Drenttel Doyle Partners*
CLIENT *American Center for Design*

Peace on Earth

Vertical Butt Stroke to groin.

Season's Greetings

Smash to face.

Happy Holidays

Jab to throat.

Silver Medalist/National

POSTER, OTHER THAN ADVERTISING, SERIES
Holiday Posters
ART DIRECTOR *Todd Fedell*
CREATIVE DIRECTOR *Russ Haan*
DESIGNER *Todd Fedell*
COPYWRITER *Russ Haan*
ILLUSTRATOR *U.S. Marine Corps*
AGENCY *After Hours Creative*
CLIENT *Vent*

Oh, horrors'

Tony Magistrale is upset. It's a woozily humid mid-August morning, the last day of summer classes, and the University of Vermont professor of English, midway through his final lecture, has just been thrown a curve.

"Do you know what my problem is with your class, Professor Magistrale?" asks a young student, as she nervously pulls on the brim of her baseball cap. "I'm getting no respect for taking it. When I go to the library for books, people ask me why I'm reading this, this . . . trash."

Magistrale understands. In fact, during the six years he has taught this course, he has grown used to such rude questioning himself. Called in its present form "The Films and Novels of Stephen King," it compares the best-selling horror novelist to many of the masters of American literature. Most frustrating is the fact that many of his critics have never even read King's work. "I always want to reply, 'Get off your high horse. Don't pretend you're Mr. or Mrs. Elitist,'" Magistrale tells the student. "King is a contemporary Faulkner or Dickens. His work touches on great themes. He just happens to be a more accessible writer."

Dwight Garner is a free-lance writer who lives in New York City.

The young woman brightens, as do the other students in the class. Heads nod in agreement. Later, another student says: "Maybe I can get my dad to read *The Stand.* Then he'll understand."

AT AGE 42, TONY MAGISTRALE IS AMERIca's leading Stephen King scholar – a man who has spent the past decade trying (and usually failing) to get other academics to understand his passion for the man from Belfast, Maine. Nor is Magistrale alone in his ardor. He's at the forefront of a group of several dozen academics who teach and analyze King's books with the same rigor that previous generations of scholars brought to, say, *The Divine Comedy* or *The Iliad.*

Thanks to these enthusiasts, there are now more books about Stephen King's work (roughly 50) than there are books by King himself (34). And at schools like the University of Vermont, in Burlington, where Magistrale has taught a class on King since 1988, students are rushing to enroll. When more than 40 students signed up for his course this past summer, Magistrale was forced to add a second section.

The term "Stephen King scholar" may sound like an *Continued on Page 22*

Some argue that Stephen King is the Charles Dickens of our day. Others say his work has no place in a college curriculum.
By Dwight Garner

ILLUSTRATION BY RALPH GIGUERE **15**

Distinctive Merit/National

FULL PAGE OR SPREAD
Oh, Horrors
ART DIRECTOR *Lucy Bartholomay*
CREATIVE DIRECTOR *Lucy Bartholomay*
DESIGNER *Lucy Bartholomay*
ILLUSTRATOR *Ralph Giguere*
CLIENT *The Boston Globe*

Distinctive Merit/National

COVER
The Arab Paradox
ART DIRECTOR *Lucy Bartholomay*
CREATIVE DIRECTOR *Lucy Bartholomay*
DESIGNER *Lucy Bartholomay*
ILLUSTRATOR *Brian Cronin*
CLIENT *The Boston Globe*

Distinctive Merit/National

COVER
Here's Looking at You. Kids
ART DIRECTOR *Lucy Bartholomay*
CREATIVE DIRECTOR *Lucy Bartholomay*
DESIGNER *Lucy Bartholomay*
ILLUSTRATOR *Scott Menchin*
CLIENT *The Boston Globe*

Distinctive Merit/International

MULTIPAGE
Cut, September Issue
ART DIRECTOR *Hideki Nakajima*
DESIGNERS *Hideki Nakajima, Yuko Kasuga,*
Iwao Miura, Masashi Nakayama,
Kenichi Kawakami
EDITOR IN CHIEF *Ken Sato*
PHOTOGRAPHERS *Bruce Weber, Herb Ritts,*
Yoram Kahana, Douglas Kirkland
CLIENT *Rockin'on Inc.*

特集「タンゴ」
愚かしくも愛しい、フランス式男と女の愛の狂騒劇

Distinctive Merit/International

MULTIPAGE
Cut, March Issue
ART DIRECTOR *Hideki Nakajima*
DESIGNERS *Hideki Nakajima, Yuko Kasuga,
Iwao Miura, Masashi Nakayama,
Kenichi Kawakami*
EDITOR IN CHIEF *Ken Sato*
PHOTOGRAPHERS *Luc Roux, Albert Watson,
Kurt Markus*
CLIENT *Rockin'on Inc.*

女優ってまるでリュックを背負って国から国を渡り歩く旅人のようだわ。
つねに新たな問いかけが生まれ、終わりがないの。

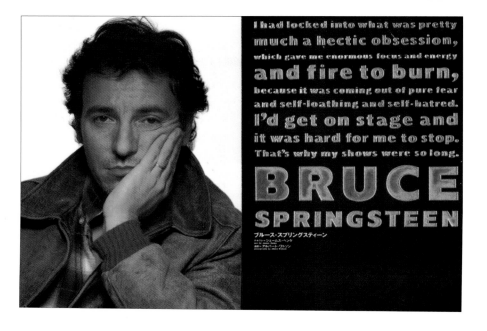

I had locked into what was pretty much a hectic obsession, which gave me enormous focus and energy and fire to burn, because it was coming out of pure fear and self-loathing and self-hatred. I'd get on stage and it was hard for me to stop. That's why my shows were so long.

BRUCE SPRINGSTEEN

Distinctive Merit/National

FULL ISSUE
Generation Next
CREATIVE DIRECTOR *Fred Woodward*
DESIGNERS *Fred Woodward, Gail Anderson,*
Geraldine Hessler, Lee Bearson
PHOTO EDITORS *Jodi Peckman, Denise Sfraga*
PHOTOGRAPHERS *Various*
CLIENT *Rolling Stone*

ADDITIONAL AWARD

Merit
COVER

Distinctive Merit/International

FULL ISSUES
Dogs Issue, Paper Game Issue, Swiss Cross and
Passport Issue
ART DIRECTORS *Karin Bolliger, Barbara Erb,*
Lukas Huggenberg, Urs Arnold
CREATIVE DIRECTOR *Urs Arnold*
DESIGNERS *Karin Bolliger (Dogs), Lukas Huggenberg*
(Paper Game), Barbara Erb (Swiss Cross and
Passport)
PHOTOGRAPHER *Mathias Hofstetter*
AGENCY *Arnold Design Switzerland*
CLIENT *Canon/Walter Rentsh AG, Switzerland*

(facing page)
Distinctive Merit/National

HOUSE PUBLICATION, SINGLE ISSUE
Interact: American Center for Design Journal
ART DIRECTOR *Eric Wagner*
DESIGNERS *Grant Davis, Anthony Ma,*
Lance Rutter, Eric Wagner
ILLUSTRATOR *Eric Wagner*
STUDIO *Tanagram*
CLIENT *American Center for Design*

interact american center for design journal

TEXTS & DOCUMENTS

EMPATHY, FORM, AND SPACE

PROBLEMS IN GERMAN AESTHETICS,
1873–1893

Robert Vischer
1873

Conrad Fiedler
1878

Heinrich Wölfflin
1886

Adolf Göller
1887

Adolf Hildebrand
1893

August Schmarsow
1893

INTRODUCTION AND TRANSLATION
BY HARRY FRANCIS MALLGRAVE AND ELEFTHERIOS IKONOMOU

Distinctive Merit/National

SINGLE
Sarah McLachlan Book
ART DIRECTORS *Susan Mendola, Angela Skouras*
CREATIVE DIRECTOR *Susan Mendola*
DESIGNER *Angela Skouras*
COPYWRITER *Michael Schwartz*
PHOTOGRAPHERS *Dennis Keeley, Kharen Hill,
David Atlas*
ILLUSTRATOR *Sarah McLachlan*

Distinctive Merit/National

SINGLE
*Empathy, Form, and Space: Problems in German
Aesthetics, 1873–1893*
DESIGNER *Laurie Haycock Makela*
STUDIO *J. Paul Getty Trust, Publication Services*
CLIENT *The Getty Center for the History of Art
and the Humanities*

(facing page, top)
Distinctive Merit/National

SINGLE
*This Heritage Remembered VI: O. Henry:
One Dozen Stories*
ART DIRECTOR *Lana Rigsby*
SERIES DIRECTOR *Robert J. Downs, Jr.*
DESIGNERS *Lana Rigsby, Michael Thede,
Troy S. Ford*
PROLOGUE AUTHOR *JoAnn Stone*
PHOTOGRAPHER *Geof Kern*
ILLUSTRATOR *Michael Thede*
STUDIO *Rigsby Design, Inc.*
CLIENT *Heritage Press*

(facing page, bottom)
Distinctive Merit/National

SINGLE
Pat Hackett Christmas Card 1993
ART DIRECTOR *Janet Kruse*
CREATIVE DIRECTOR *Janet Kruse*
DESIGNER *Traci Daberko*
AGENCY *The Leonhardt Group*
STUDIO *The Leonhardt Group*
CLIENT *Pat Hackett, Artist Representative*

(facing page, top left)
Distinctive Merit/International

SINGLE
Graphis Products by Design 1
ART DIRECTOR *B. Martin Pedersen*
CREATIVE DIRECTOR *B. Martin Pedersen*
DESIGNER *B. Martin Pedersen*
STUDIO *Pedersen Design Inc.*
CLIENT *Graphis*

(facing page, top right)
Distinctive Merit/International

SINGLE
Graphis Packaging 6
ART DIRECTOR *B. Martin Pedersen*
CREATIVE DIRECTOR *B. Martin Pedersen*
DESIGNER *B. Martin Pedersen*
STUDIO *Pedersen Design Inc.*
CLIENT *Graphis*

ADDITIONAL AWARD

Distinctive Merit
BOOK JACKET, SINGLE

(facing page, bottom left)
Distinctive Merit/International

SINGLE
Graphis Design 95
ART DIRECTOR *B. Martin Pedersen*
CREATIVE DIRECTOR *B. Martin Pedersen*
DESIGNER *B. Martin Pedersen*
PHOTOGRAPHER *Albert Zimmerman*
STUDIO *Pedersen Design Inc.*
CLIENT *Graphis*

ADDITIONAL AWARD

Distinctive Merit
BOOK JACKET, SINGLE

(facing page, bottom right)
Distinctive Merit/International

SINGLE
Graphis Brochures 1
ART DIRECTOR *B. Martin Pedersen*
CREATIVE DIRECTOR *B. Martin Pedersen*
DESIGNER *B. Martin Pedersen*
STUDIO *Pedersen Design Inc.*
CLIENT *Graphis*

ADDITIONAL AWARD

Distinctive Merit
BOOK JACKET, SINGLE

Distinctive Merit/National

SERIES
Do It! Guides
ART DIRECTOR *Michael Bierut*
DESIGNERS *Michael Bierut, Agnethe Glatved*
PHOTOGRAPHER *John Paul Endress*
ILLUSTRATOR *Nicholas Fasciano*
STUDIO *Pentagram Design*
CLIENT *Redefinition Books*

Distinctive Merit/National

TITLE FOR PROMOTION, SINGLE
News Weasels Show Open
ART DIRECTOR *Jill Taffet*
CREATIVE DIRECTOR *Jill Taffet*
DESIGNER *Mark Osborne*
PRODUCER *Karin Rainey*
DIRECTOR *Mark Osborne*
MUSIC *John Wiggins*
STUDIO *E! Entertainment Television*
CLIENT *E! Entertainment Television*

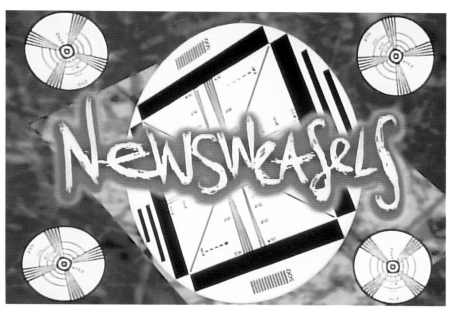

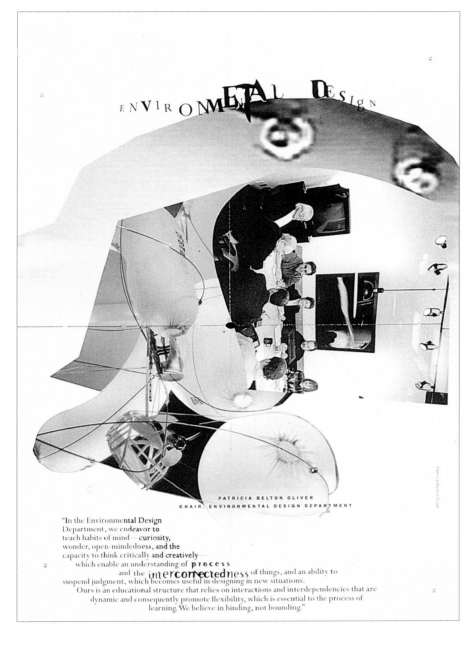

BOOKLET, FOLDER, OR BROCHURE, SINGLE
Masterworks Two
ART DIRECTOR *Michael Bierut*
DESIGNERS *Michael Bierut, Esther Bridavsky*
PHOTOGRAPHERS *Various*
STUDIO *Pentagram Design*
CLIENT *Peter Joseph Gallery*

(facing page, bottom)
Distinctive Merit/National

BOOKLET, FOLDER, OR BROCHURE, SINGLE
Vernon Fisher Exhibition Catalogue
ART DIRECTOR *Renate Gokl*
DESIGNER *Renate Gokl*
COPYWRITER *Buzz Spector*
PHOTOGRAPHER *Vernon Fisher*
CLIENT *Krannert Art Museum*

Distinctive Merit/National

BOOKLET, FOLDER, OR BROCHURE, SINGLE
Art Center College of Design Catalogue 1995–96
DESIGN DIRECTOR *Rebeca Méndez*
CREATIVE DIRECTOR *Stuart I. Frolick*
DESIGNER *Darin Beaman*
ASSOCIATE DESIGNER *Chris Haaga*
EDITOR *Julie Suhr*
PHOTOGRAPHER *Steven A. Heller*
STUDIO *Art Center Design Office*
CLIENT *Art Center College of Design*

Distinctive Merit/International

BOOKLET, FOLDER, OR BROCHURE, SINGLE
Directions Spring and Summer '94
ART DIRECTOR *Benny Lau*
CREATIVE DIRECTOR *Steve Meltzer*
DESIGNER *Benny Lau*
COPYWRITER *Fiona Upward*
ILLUSTRATORS *Michael McKeever, Dee Dee Choy*
AGENCY *J. Walter Thompson Direct, Hong Kong*
CLIENT *The Swank Shop*

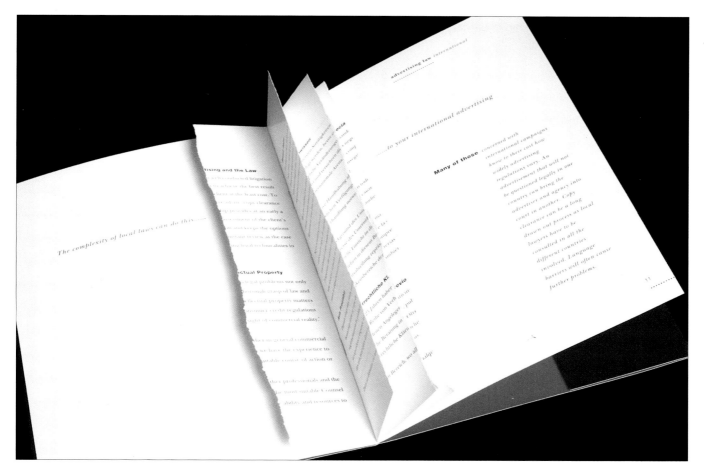

Distinctive Merit/International

BOOKLET, FOLDER, OR BROCHURE, SINGLE
Advertising Law International Brochure
CREATIVE DIRECTORS *Lynn Trickett, Brian Webb*
DESIGNERS *Lynn Trickett, Brian Webb,
Steve Edwards*
COPYWRITER *Neil Mattingley*
CLIENT *The Simkins Partnership*

Distinctive Merit/International

BOOKLET, FOLDER, OR BROCHURE, SINGLE
James Yunker Spring and Summer 1994
ART DIRECTOR *Del Terrelonge*
PHOTOGRAPHER *Shin Sugino*
AGENCY *Terrelonge*
CLIENT *James Yunker*

Distinctive Merit/International

BOOKLET, FOLDER, OR BROCHURE, SINGLE
The Czech Technology Park, Brno
CREATIVE DIRECTOR *Michael Denny*
DESIGNERS *John Bateson, Rachael Dinnis,*
Jonathan Simpson
PHOTOGRAPHERS *Tim Flach, Damien Gillie*
CLIENT *The Czech Technology Park, Brno*

Distinctive Merit/International

BOOKLET, FOLDER, OR BROCHURE, SINGLE
Fliessender Verkehr
ART DIRECTOR *Franz Merlicek*
CREATIVE DIRECTOR *Franz Merlicek*
GRAPHICS *Tina Feiertag*
COPYWRITER *Stefan Pott*
PRODUCER *Werner Stupka*
AGENCY *Demner & Merlicek*
CLIENT *Rhenus AG*

Distinctive Merit/International

PACKAGING, SERIES
Leisure Spanish Olives
CREATIVE DIRECTOR *Robin Hall*
DESIGNER *Barry Gillibrand*
ILLUSTRATOR *Bob Haberfield*
CLIENT *Leisure Fine Food & Drinks Ltd.*

Distinctive Merit/International

PACKAGING, SERIES
Studio NOB Envelope
ART DIRECTOR *Akio Okumura*
DESIGNER *Katsuji Minami*
STUDIO *Packaging Create Inc.*
CLIENT *Studio NOB*

Distinctive Merit/National

ANNOUNCEMENT, INVITATION, OR MENU, SINGLE
Subpoena
ART DIRECTOR *Tony Pucca*
CREATIVE DIRECTOR *Tim Fisher*
DESIGNER *John Cason*
COPYWRITER *Tony Pucca*
ILLUSTRATOR *Mariel Llenza*
AGENCY *Fry Hammond Barr*
CLIENT *The Creative Club of Orlando*

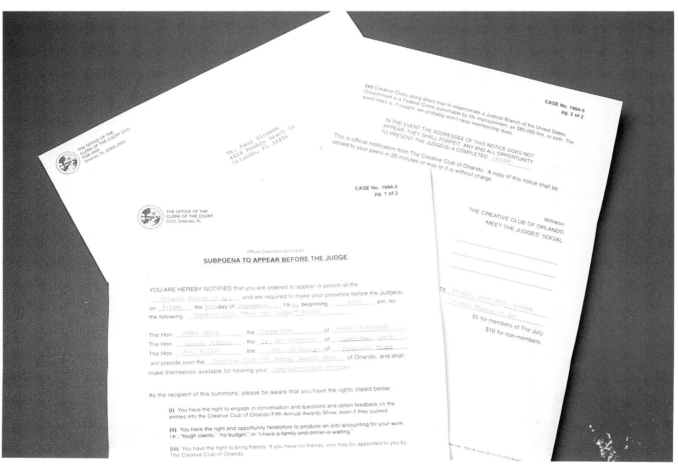

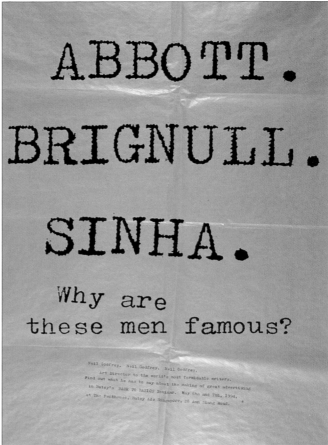

(facing page)
Distinctive Merit/International

ANNOUNCEMENT, INVITATION, OR MENU, SERIES
Batey Back to Basics Seminar
ART DIRECTOR *Eddie Wong*
CREATIVE DIRECTOR *Jim Aitchison*
DESIGNER *Eddie Wong*
COPYWRITERS *Sim Yang Seah, Jim Aitchison*
AGENCY *Batey Ads Singapore*
CLIENT *Batey Ads Singapore*

(above)
Distinctive Merit/National

CALENDAR OR APPOINTMENT BOOK
A Literary Book of Days
ART DIRECTOR *Louise Fili*
CREATIVE DIRECTOR *Louise Fili*
DESIGNERS *Louise Fili, Leah Lococo*
STUDIO *Louise Fili Ltd.*
CLIENT *Crown Publishing*

Distinctive Merit/National

CALENDAR OR APPOINTMENT BOOK
Elements of Time
ART DIRECTOR *Michael McGinn*
CREATIVE DIRECTOR *James A. Sebastian*
DESIGNERS *James A. Sebastian, Frank Nichols*
STUDIO *Designframe Inc.*
CLIENT *Strathmore Paper Co.*

Distinctive Merit/International

LOGO OR TRADEMARK
Dialog Logo
ART DIRECTOR *Peter Smith*
CREATIVE DIRECTOR *Peter Smith*
DESIGNER *Peter Smith*
STUDIO *Dialog Limited*

Distinctive Merit/International

LOGO OR TRADEMARK
London Radio Logo
ART DIRECTOR *John Rushworth*
CREATIVE DIRECTOR *John Rushworth*
DESIGNERS *John Rushworth, Nick Finney*
COPYWRITER *David Gibbs*
PHOTOGRAPHER *Phil Sayer*
STUDIO *Pentagram Design Ltd.*
CLIENT *London Radio Services Ltd.*

Distinctive Merit/National

LETTERHEAD, BUSINESS CARD, ENVELOPE
Acme Advertising Stationery
ART DIRECTOR *Sakol Mongkolkasetarin*
CREATIVE DIRECTOR *Sakol Mongkolkasetarin*
DESIGNER *Sakol Mongkolkasetarin*
COPYWRITER *Brian West*
ILLUSTRATOR *Sakol Mongkolkasetarin*
AGENCY *Acme Advertising*
CLIENT *Acme Advertising*

Distinctive Merit/National

LETTERHEAD, BUSINESS CARD, ENVELOPE
Donald M. Ward, C.P.A.
ART DIRECTOR *Patrick Short*
DESIGNER *Patrick Short*
PHOTOGRAPHER *Alex Bee*
STUDIO *BlackBird Creative*
CLIENT *Donald M. Ward, C.P.A.*

(facing page)
Distinctive Merit/National

CORPORATE IDENTITY PROGRAM
The Public Theater
ART DIRECTOR *Paula Scher*
DESIGNERS *Ron Louie, Lisa Mazur, Paula Scher*
STUDIO *Pentagram Design*
CLIENT *The Public Theater*

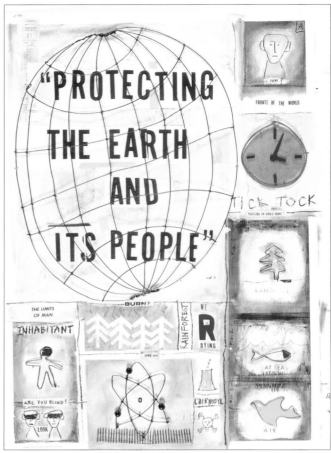

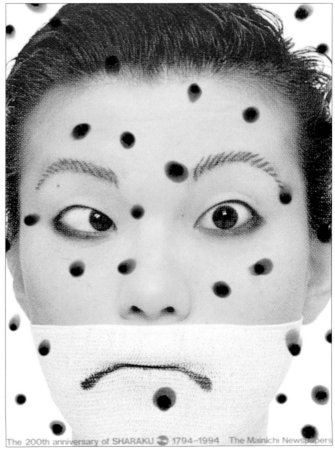

Distinctive Merit/National

POSTER, OTHER THAN ADVERTISING, SINGLE
Day by Day
ART DIRECTOR *Neil Powell*
CREATIVE DIRECTOR *Neil Powell*
DESIGNER *Neil Powell*
ILLUSTRATOR *Neil Powell*
STUDIO *Duffy Design*
CLIENT *Graphic Communication Society of Oklahoma*

Distinctive Merit/National

POSTER, OTHER THAN ADVERTISING, SINGLE
World Conservation
ART DIRECTORS *Team*
CREATIVE DIRECTOR *Joe Duffy*
DESIGNER *Neil Powell*
STUDIO *Duffy Design*
CLIENT *World Conservation*

Distinctive Merit/International

POSTER, OTHER THAN ADVERTISING, SINGLE
The 200th Anniversary of Sharaku
ART DIRECTOR *Koji Mizutani*
CREATIVE DIRECTOR *Koji Mizutani*
DESIGNER *Hiroshi Ohmizo*
PHOTOGRAPHER *Yoshihiko Ueda*
STUDIO *Mizutani Studio*
CLIENT *The Mainichi Newspapers*

(facing page)
Distinctive Merit/International

POSTER, OTHER THAN ADVERTISING, SERIES
LIFE
ART DIRECTOR *Shin Matsunaga*
DESIGNER *Shin Matsunaga*
ILLUSTRATOR *Shin Matsunaga*
STUDIO *Shin Matsunaga Design Inc.*
CLIENT *Japan Design Committee*

(above)
Distinctive Merit/National

SELF-PROMOTION, SINGLE
Louise Fili Ltd. Promotion
ART DIRECTOR *Louise Fili*
CREATIVE DIRECTOR *Louise Fili*
DESIGNER *Louise Fili*
COPYWRITER *Steven Heller*
PHOTOGRAPHERS *Ed Spiro, David Barry*
STUDIO *Louise Fili Ltd.*
CLIENT *Louise Fili Ltd.*

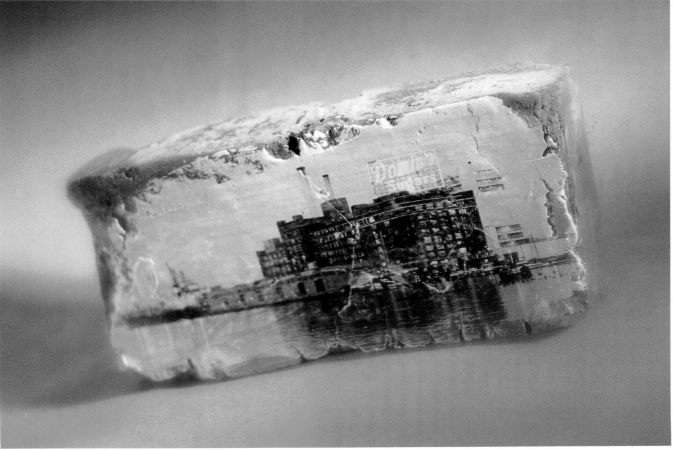

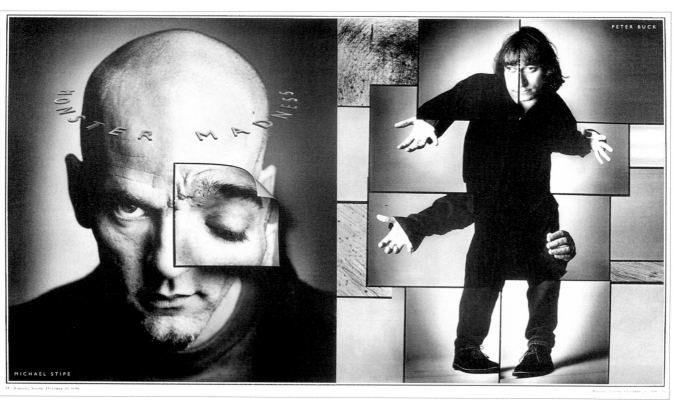

Merit/National

FULL ISSUE
Upper and Lower Case, Vol. 21.1, Summer 1994
ART DIRECTORS *Woody Pirtle, John Klotnia*
DESIGNERS *Woody Pirtle, John Klotnia,*
Ivette Montes de Oca
STUDIO *Pentagram Design*
CLIENT *International Typeface Corporation*

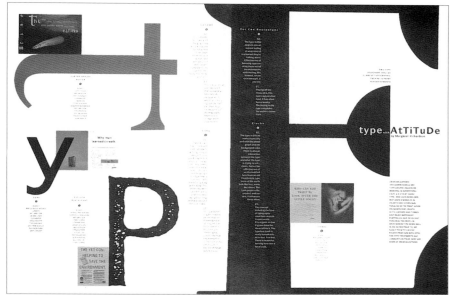

Merit/National

FULL ISSUE
Upper and Lower Case, Vol. 21.3, Winter 1994
ART DIRECTORS *Woody Pirtle, John Klotnia*
DESIGNERS *Ivette Montes de Oca, Robert Spica*
STUDIO *Pentagram Design*
CLIENT *International Typeface Corporation*

(facing page, top)
Merit/International

FULL ISSUE
Baseline 17
ART DIRECTOR *Hans Dieter Reichert*
CREATIVE DIRECTOR *Hans Dieter Reichert*
DESIGNER *Hans Dieter Reichert*
DESIGN ASSISTANT *Brian Cunningham*
EDITOR *Mike Daines*
PHOTOGRAPHERS *Everald Williams,
Hans Dieter Reichert*
STUDIO *HDR Design*
CLIENT *Letraset Esselte*

(facing page, bottom)
Merit/International

FULL ISSUE
P Magazine, Issue 9
ART DIRECTOR *John Rushworth*
CREATIVE DIRECTOR *John Rushworth*
DESIGNERS *John Rushworth, Chiew Yong*
COPYWRITER *Renato Broglia*
PHOTOGRAPHERS *Various*
STUDIO *Pentagram Design Ltd.*
CLIENT *Polaroid Corporation*

Merit/National

MULTIPLE ISSUES
ZiNj Number 2, ZiNj Number 3
ART DIRECTOR *David Volsic*
CREATIVE DIRECTORS *David Volsic, Debra Harris*
DESIGNERS *David Volsic, Sheryl Lundgreen,
Heidi Shelley*
COPYWRITERS *Kevin Jones, Debra Harris*
PHOTOGRAPHERS *Murray Close, Chip Clark,
Kevin Jones*
ILLUSTRATORS *David Volsic,
Carl P. Brest Van Kampen, Mark Hallet*
AGENCY *Harris.Volsic Creative*
CLIENT *Interagency Task Force*

Merit/National

FULL ISSUE
Rough, March
ART DIRECTORS *Chuck Johnson, Ken Koester*
CREATIVE DIRECTOR *Chuck Johnson*
DESIGNERS *Chuck Johnson, Ken Koester, Rob Smith*
EDITORS *Margie Bowles, Phil Hollenbeck*
COPYWRITERS *Margie Bowles, Phil Hollenbeck,*
George Toomer, Max Wright
PHOTOGRAPHER *Phil Hollenbeck*
ILLUSTRATORS *Chuck Johnson, Ken Koester*
STUDIO *Brainstorm, Inc.*
CLIENT *Dallas Society of Visual Communication*

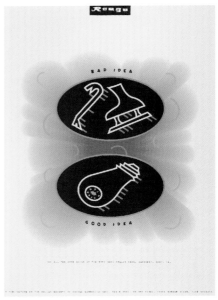

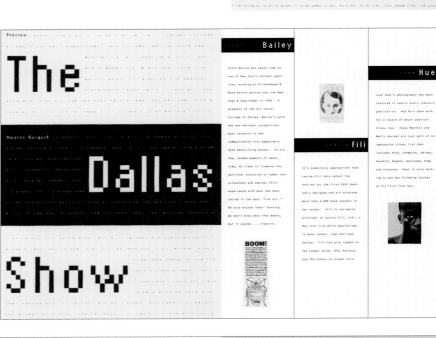

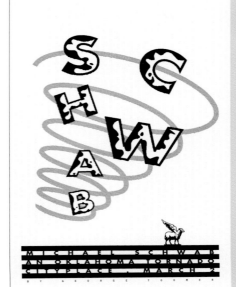

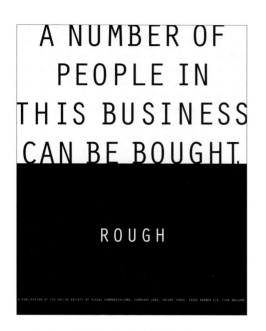

A NUMBER OF
PEOPLE IN
THIS BUSINESS
CAN BE BOUGHT.

ROUGH

Merit/National

FULL ISSUE
Rough, February
ART DIRECTORS *Chuck Johnson, Ken Koester*
CREATIVE DIRECTOR *Chuck Johnson*
DESIGNERS *Chuck Johnson, Ken Koester, Rob Smith*
EDITORS *Margie Bowles, Phil Hollenbeck*
COPYWRITERS *Margie Bowles, Phil Hollenbeck,*
Ken Koester
PHOTOGRAPHERS *Greg Watermann, Kent Kirkley*
STUDIO *Brainstorm, Inc.*
CLIENT *Dallas Society of Visual Communication*

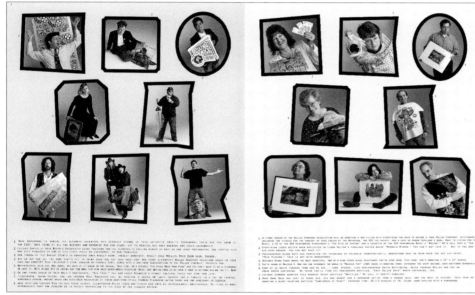

Merit/National

SINGLE
A History of Women Photographers
ART DIRECTOR *Monika Keano*
DESIGNER *Joyce Rothschild*
AUTHOR *Naomi Rosenblum*
CLIENT *Abbeville Press*

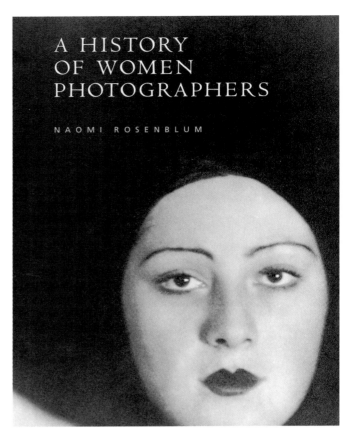

Merit/National

SINGLE
ABC
ART DIRECTOR *Stephen Doyle*
DESIGNER *Gary Tooth*
AUTHOR *William Wegman*
PHOTOGRAPHER *William Wegman*
STUDIO *Drenttel Doyle Partners*
CLIENT *Hyperion Books for Children*

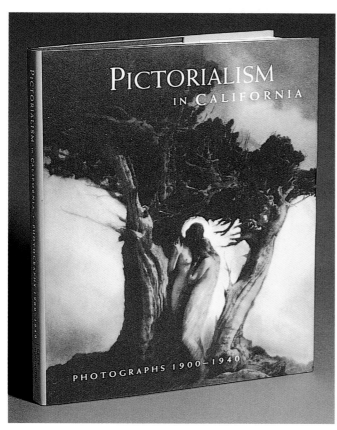

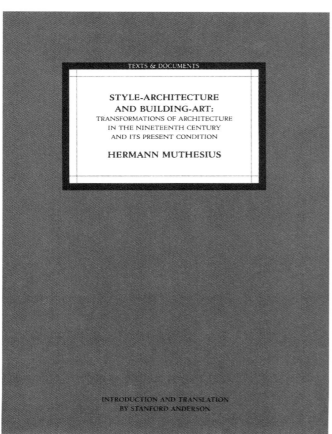

Merit/National

SINGLE
Pictorialism in California
DESIGNER *Kurt Hauser*
STUDIO *J. Paul Getty Trust, Publication Services*
CLIENT *J. Paul Getty Museum*

Merit/National

SINGLE
Style-Architecture and Building-Art: Transformations of Architecture in the Nineteenth Century and Its Present Condition
DESIGNER *Lorraine Wild*
AUTHOR *Hermann Muthesius*
STUDIO *J. Paul Getty Trust, Publication Services*
CLIENT *The Getty Center for the History of Art and the Humanities*

Merit/National

SINGLE
This Heritage Remembered V: Shakespeare
ART DIRECTOR *Woody Pirtle*
CREATIVE DIRECTOR *Woody Pirtle*
DESIGNERS *Woody Pirtle, John Klotnia, Ivette Montes de Oca*
COPYWRITER *Lee Herrick*
ILLUSTRATOR *Anthony Russo*
PRODUCER *Bob Downs*
STUDIO *Pentagram Design*
CLIENT *Heritage Press*

Merit/National

SINGLE
Bra Fashions by Stephanie
ART DIRECTOR *Seymour Chwast*
CREATIVE DIRECTOR *Seymour Chwast*
DESIGNER *Seymour Chwast*
COPYWRITER *Seymour Chwast*
ILLUSTRATOR *Seymour Chwast*
STUDIO *The Pushpin Group, Inc.*
CLIENT *Warner Books*

(facing page, top)
Merit/National

SINGLE
Roy Lichtenstein
ART DIRECTOR *Takaaki Matsumoto*
CREATIVE DIRECTOR *Takaaki Matsumoto*
DESIGNER *Takaaki Matsumoto*
MANAGING EDITOR *Anthony Calnek*
AUTHOR *Diane Waldman*
PHOTOGRAPHERS *Various*
STUDIO *Matsumoto Incorporated*
CLIENT *Solomon R. Guggenheim Museum*

(facing page, bottom)
Merit/National

SINGLE
Wildlife
ART DIRECTOR *John Ball*
CREATIVE DIRECTOR *John Ball*
DESIGNERS *John Ball, Gale Spitzley*
COPYWRITER *Reesey Shaw*
AGENCY *Mires Design, Inc.*
STUDIO *Mires Design, Inc.*
CLIENT *California Center for the Arts Museum*

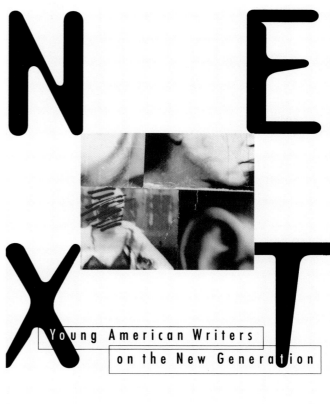

NEXT

Young American Writers
on the New Generation

edited by **ERIC LIU**

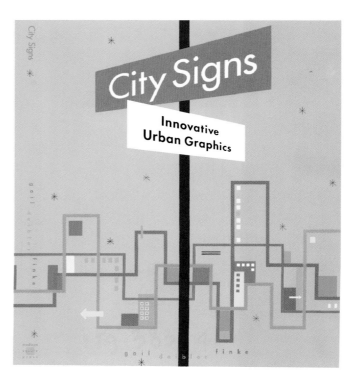

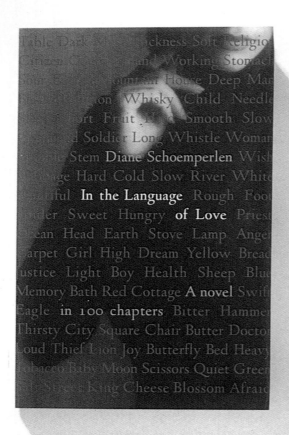

Merit/International

SINGLE
In the Language of Love
ART DIRECTORS *John Pylypczak, Diti Katona*
DESIGNERS *John Pylypczak, Renata Chubb*
PHOTOGRAPHER *Karen Levy*
STUDIO *Concrete Design Communications Inc.*
CLIENT *Harper Collins*

  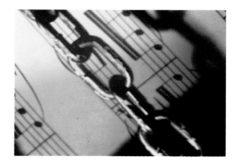

Merit/National

TITLE FOR PROMOTION, SINGLE
Saturday Night Live 20th-Anniversary Opening
DESIGNERS *John Dire, Michael Riley*
SPECIAL-EFFECTS EDITOR *Burtis Scott*
PHOTOGRAPHERS *Sheila Metzner (still photography),*
Toby Phillips (live-action photography)
PRODUCERS *R/Greenberg Associates,*
Savoy Commercials, NBC Productions
DIRECTORS *Toby Phillips, Jim Signorelli*
CLIENT *NBC/Saturday Night Live*

Merit/International

TITLE FOR PROMOTION, SINGLE
Super Saturday
ART DIRECTOR *Yasutaka Taga*
PHOTOGRAPHER *Yutaka Nozaki*
ILLUSTRATOR *Yasutaka Taga*
DIRECTOR *Shingo Kiritani*
AGENCY *Yasutaka Taga*
CLIENT *Kitanihon Broadcasting*

Merit/National

TITLE FOR PROMOTION, CAMPAIGN
VH1 Darcy's Music Packaging
ART DIRECTOR *Rob Grobengieser*
CREATIVE DIRECTOR *Lauren Zalaznick*
DESIGNERS *Anne Marie Gilligan, Thomas Gallagher*
PRODUCER *Rob Grobengieser*
DIRECTOR *Rob Grobengieser*
CLIENT *VH1*

Merit/National

TITLE FOR PROMOTION, CAMPAIGN
VH1 Top-Ten Packaging
CREATIVE DIRECTOR *Lauren Zalaznick*
PRODUCER *Jon Klein*
DIRECTORS *Bill Price, Chris Weinstein*
AGENCY *Optic Nerve*
CLIENT *VH1*

Merit/International

TITLE FOR PROMOTION, CAMPAIGN
TV Addicts (Channel 4 Presentations, Attention Grabbers)
ART DIRECTOR *Steve White*
CREATIVE DIRECTOR *Glenn Carwithen*
DESIGNER *Glenn Carwithen*
COPYWRITER *Glenn Carwithen*
PRODUCER *Charlie Druce*
DIRECTOR *Glenn Carwithen*
MUSIC *Nick Berry, Moulinaire SFX*
STUDIO *Brewers Production and Post-Production*
CLIENT *Channel 4*

Merit/National

SPECIAL EFFECTS AND COMPUTER GRAPHICS, SINGLE
Delivery
ART DIRECTORS *Rick Hansen, Russell Sinclair*
CREATIVE DIRECTOR *Charlie Miesmer*
COPYWRITERS *Ted Cohn, Peter Smith, Jimmy Segal*
COMPUTER GRAPHICS *R/Greenberg Associates*
PRODUCERS *Steve and Linda Horn Productions,*
R/Greenberg Associates
POST-PRODUCTION *R/Greenberg Associates*
DIRECTOR *Steve Horn*
MUSIC *Maverick Music*
AGENCY *BBDO New York*
CLIENT *Pizza Hut*

Merit/National

ANIMATION, SINGLE
Buy Low, Buy Lower
ART DIRECTOR *Bob Hoffman*
CREATIVE DIRECTOR *Bob Hoffman*
DESIGNER *David Levine*
COPYWRITER *Jay Courtney*
ILLUSTRATOR *David Levine*
PRODUCER *J. J. Sedelmaier*
DIRECTOR *J. J. Sedelmaier*
MUSIC *Shapiro*
AGENCY *Gearon/Hoffman*
STUDIO *J. J. Sedelmaier Productions, Inc.*
CLIENT *Brown & Company*

Merit/National

CAMPAIGN
JBL OnBoard
ART DIRECTOR *Jane Brady*
CREATIVE DIRECTOR *Christian Uhl*
DESIGNER *Ben Segal*
COPYWRITER *Mike Mooney*
PHOTOGRAPHER *Mark Steele*
STUDIO *Fitch Inc.*
CLIENT *JBL Consumer Products*

(facing page)
Merit/International

CAMPAIGN
Shin-Yokohama Raumen Museum
ART DIRECTOR *Takanori Aiba*
DESIGNER *G & D*
PRODUCER *Takanori Aiba*
DIRECTOR *Takanori Aiba*
CLIENT *Shin-Yokohama Raumen Museum*

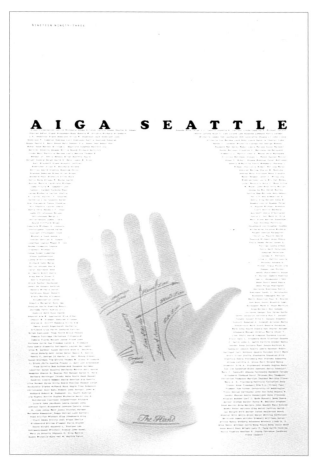

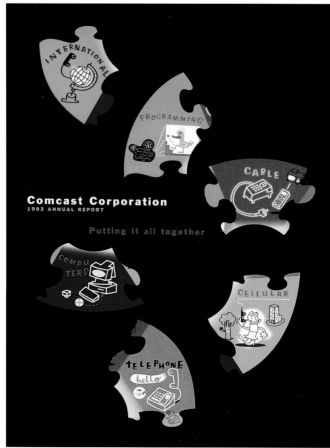

Merit/National

ANNUAL REPORT
AIGA, Seattle 1993 Annual Report
ART DIRECTOR *John Van Dyke*
CREATIVE DIRECTOR *John Van Dyke*
DESIGNER *John Van Dyke*
COPYWRITER *Karen Wilson*
PHOTOGRAPHER *Abrams/Lacagnina*
STUDIO *Van Dyke Company*
CLIENT *AIGA, Seattle*

Merit/National

ANNUAL REPORT
Comcast Corporation 1993 Annual Report
CREATIVE DIRECTORS *Aubrey Balkind, Kent Hunter*
DESIGNER *Kin Yuen*
COPYWRITERS *Michael Clive, Comcast Corporation*
PHOTOGRAPHERS *Various*
ILLUSTRATOR *J. Otto Siebold*
AGENCY *Frankfurt Balkind Partners*
CLIENT *Comcast Corporation*

Merit/National

ANNUAL REPORT
Sigma Circuits Annual Report 1994
ART DIRECTORS *George Mimnaugh, Joan Libera*
CREATIVE DIRECTOR *Joan Libera*
DESIGNER *George Mimnaugh*
ILLUSTRATOR *Marvin Mattelson*
STUDIO *Libera and Associates*
CLIENT *Sigma Circuits, Inc.*

ANNUAL REPORT
ICOS Corporation 1993 Annual Report
ART DIRECTOR *John Van Dyke*
CREATIVE DIRECTOR *John Van Dyke*
DESIGNERS *John Van Dyke, Ann Kumasaka*
COPYWRITERS *Tom McCarthy, ICOS Corporation*
PHOTOGRAPHER *Jeff Corwin*
ILLUSTRATOR *Stephanie Schilling*
STUDIO *Van Dyke Company*
CLIENT *ICOS Corporation*

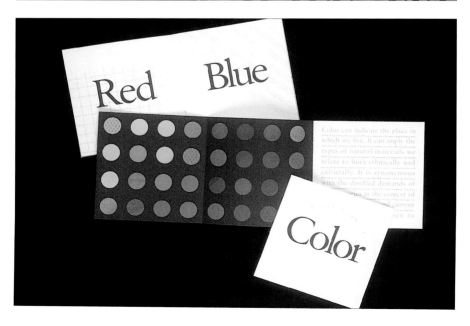

ANNUAL REPORT
BC Telecom 1993 Annual Report
ART DIRECTORS *John Van Dyke, Dave Mason*
CREATIVE DIRECTORS *John Van Dyke, Dave Mason*
DESIGNERS *John Van Dyke, Dave Mason*
COPYWRITER *Tom McCarthy*
PHOTOGRAPHER *Jim LaBounty*
STUDIO *A Design Collaborative*
CLIENT *BC Telecom*

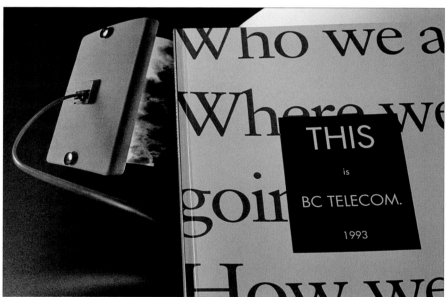

ANNUAL REPORT
Pallas Textiles In the Name of Color
ART DIRECTOR *Michael Gericke*
DESIGNERS *Donna Ching, Sharon Harel*
COPYWRITER *Maeve Slavin*
PHOTOGRAPHER *Luca Vignelli*
STUDIO *Pentagram Design*
CLIENT *Pallas Textiles*

Merit/National

ANNUAL REPORT
Success Is the One Thing No Woman Can Fake
ART DIRECTOR *Lara Gilmore*
CREATIVE DIRECTORS *Jane Talcott, Mike Rogers,*
John Staffen
COPYWRITER *Rachel Howald*
AGENCY *DDB Needham Worldwide/New York*
CLIENT *DDB Needham Worldwide/New York*

Merit/National

ANNUAL REPORT
Natural Resources Defense Council 1993
Annual Report
ART DIRECTOR *Jurek Wajdowicz*
DESIGNERS *Lisa LaRochelle, Jurek Wajdowicz*
COPYWRITERS *Emilie Trautmann,*
Kathrin Day Lassila
PHOTOGRAPHERS *Richard Elkins and others*
STUDIO *Emerson, Wajdowicz Studios, Inc.*
CLIENT *Natural Resources Defense Council*

Merit/National

ANNUAL REPORT
Molecular Dynamics 1993 Annual Report
ART DIRECTOR *Bill Cahan*
CREATIVE DIRECTOR *Bill Cahan*
DESIGNER *Bob Dinetz*
COPYWRITER *Carole Melis*
PHOTOGRAPHER *Mark Hanauer*
STUDIO *Cahan & Associates*
CLIENT *Molecular Dynamics*

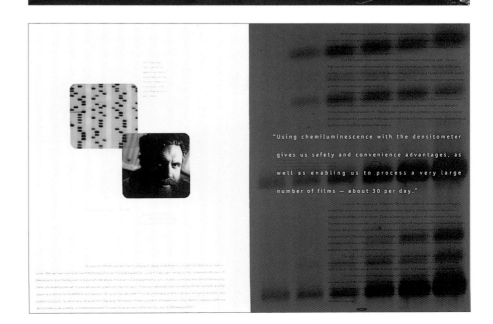

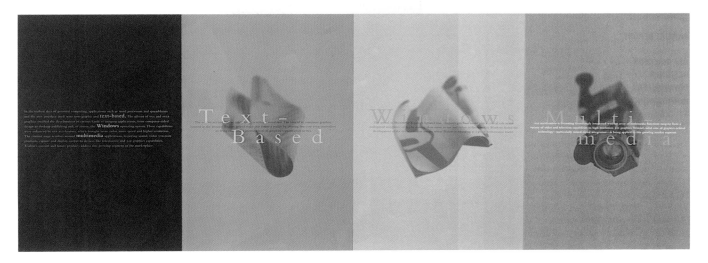

Merit/National

ANNUAL REPORT
Trident Microsystems 1994 Annual Report
ART DIRECTOR *Bill Cahan*
CREATIVE DIRECTOR *Bill Cahan*
DESIGNER *Bob Dinetz*
COPYWRITER *Tim Peters*
PHOTOGRAPHER *Holly Stewart*
STUDIO *Cahan & Associates*
CLIENT *Trident Microsystems, Inc.*

Merit/National

ANNUAL REPORT
The Limited 1993 Annual Report
CREATIVE DIRECTORS *Kent Hunter, Aubrey Balkind*
DESIGNERS *Robert Wong, Arturo Aranda*
COPYWRITER *Robert Minkoff*
PHOTOGRAPHERS *Julie Powell and others*
AGENCY *Frankfurt Balkind Partners*
CLIENT *The Limited, Inc.*

Merit/National

ANNUAL REPORT
Landmark Annual Report
ART DIRECTOR *Amy Elizabeth Farr*
CREATIVE DIRECTOR *Eric Haggman*
DESIGNER *Amy Elizabeth Farr*
COPYWRITERS *Eric Haggman, Peter Caroline*
AGENCY *Haggman Advertising*
CLIENT *Massachusetts Government Land Bank*

Merit/National

ANNUAL REPORT
1993 Houston Public Television Annual Report
ART DIRECTOR *Mark Geer*
DESIGNER *Mark Geer*
COPYWRITERS *Joe Militello, Karen Kephart*
PHOTOGRAPHY *Station Archives*
STUDIO *Geer Design, Inc.*
CLIENT *Houston Public Television*

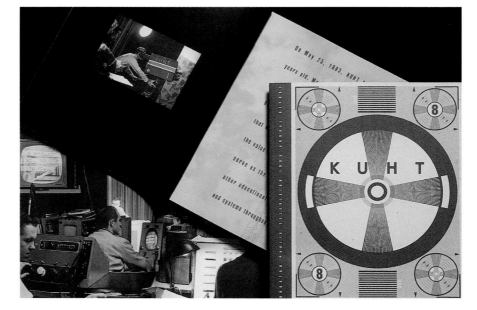

Merit/National

ANNUAL REPORT
The Rockefeller Foundation Annual Report
ART DIRECTORS *Susan Evans, Brian Sisco*
DESIGN FIRM *Sisco & Evans Ltd.*
DESIGNERS *Susan Evans, Brian Sisco*
PHOTOGRAPHERS *Jonathan Becker and others*
CLIENT *The Rockefeller Foundation*

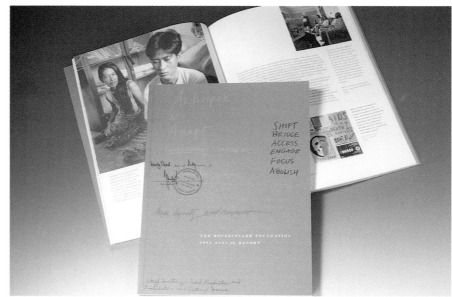

Merit/National

ANNUAL REPORT
One Company Divided
ART DIRECTOR *Steve Wedeen*
CREATIVE DIRECTOR *Steve Wedeen*
DESIGNER *Steve Wedeen*
COPYWRITER *Steve Wedeen*
PHOTOGRAPHER *Michael Barley*
STUDIO *Vaughn Wedeen Creative*
CLIENT *Lasertechnics, Inc.*

Merit/National

ANNUAL REPORT
Horizon Bank, a Savings Bank: The Fiscal 1994
Annual Report
ART DIRECTOR *Kerry Leimer*
CREATIVE DIRECTOR *Kerry Leimer*
DESIGNER *Kerry Leimer*
COPYWRITER *David Eldred*
PHOTOGRAPHER *Tyler Boley*
STUDIO *Leimer Cross Design*
CLIENT *Horizon Bank*

Merit/National

ANNUAL REPORT
Aldus Corporation 1993 Annual Report
ART DIRECTOR *Kerry Leimer*
CREATIVE DIRECTOR *Kerry Leimer*
DESIGNERS *Kerry Leimer, Craig Terrones*
COPYWRITER *Kerry Leimer*
PHOTOGRAPHER *Tyler Boley*
ILLUSTRATOR *Mark Fox*
STUDIO *Leimer Cross Design*
CLIENT *Aldus Corporation*

Merit/National

ANNUAL REPORT
Expeditors International 1993 Annual Report
ART DIRECTOR *Kerry Leimer*
CREATIVE DIRECTOR *Kerry Leimer*
DESIGNER *Kerry Leimer*
COPYWRITER *Kerry Leimer*
PHOTOGRAPHER *Tyler Boley*
STUDIO *Leimer Cross Design*
CLIENT *Expeditors International*

Merit/National

ANNUAL REPORT
ARIAD Pharmaceuticals 1993 Annual Report
ART DIRECTOR *Woody Pirtle*
DESIGNERS *John Klotnia, Ivette Montes de Oca*
PHOTOGRAPHER *Ivette Montes de Oca*
STUDIO *Pentagram Design*
CLIENT *ARIAD Pharmaceuticals*

Merit/National

ANNUAL REPORT
Portland Brewing Annual Report
ART DIRECTOR *Sally Morrow*
DESIGNER *Sally Morrow*
COPYWRITER *Portland Brewing*
PHOTOGRAPHY *Stock*
ILLUSTRATIONS *Stock*
AGENCY *Sandstrom Design*
CLIENT *Portland Brewing*

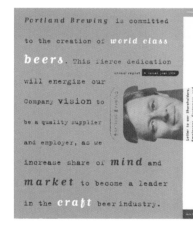

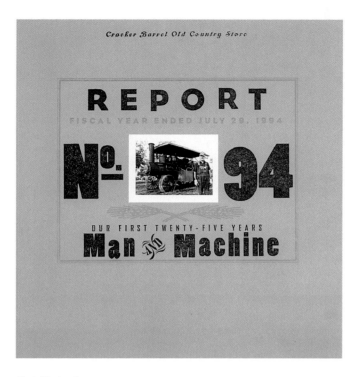

Merit/National

ANNUAL REPORT
Cracker Barrel Old Country Store
1994 Annual Report
ART DIRECTOR *Thomas Ryan*
CREATIVE DIRECTOR *Thomas Ryan*
DESIGNER *Thomas Ryan*
COPYWRITER *John Baeder*
PHOTOGRAPHER *McGuire*
ILLUSTRATOR *Paul Ritscher*
AGENCY *Corporate Communications, Inc.*
STUDIO *Thomas Ryan Design*
CLIENT *Cracker Barrel Old Country Store, Inc.*

Merit/International

ANNUAL REPORT
YMCA Annual Report
ART DIRECTORS *John Pylypczak, Diti Katona*
DESIGNERS *John Pylypczak, Renata Chubb*
PHOTOGRAPHERS *John Pylypczak, Diti Katona,*
Roman Pylypczak
STUDIO *Concrete Design Communications Inc.*
CLIENT *YMCA*

Merit/International

ANNUAL REPORT
Superior Metal Printing 1993 Annual Report
ART DIRECTOR *Craig Hutton*
CREATIVE DIRECTOR *Craig Hutton*
DESIGNER *Craig Hutton*
COPYWRITER *John Lim*
PHOTOGRAPHER *Hatty Gottschalk*
STUDIO *Su Yeang Design*
CLIENT *Superior Metal Printing*

Merit/International

ANNUAL REPORT
Annual Report 1993/1994
ART DIRECTOR *Silvio Galbucci*
CREATIVE DIRECTOR *Silvio Galbucci*
PHOTOGRAPHER *Patrick Rohner*
ILLUSTRATOR *Schnitzler Schule*
AGENCY *Matter Galbucci Leo Burnett*
CLIENT *Association of Foreign Banks in Switzerland*

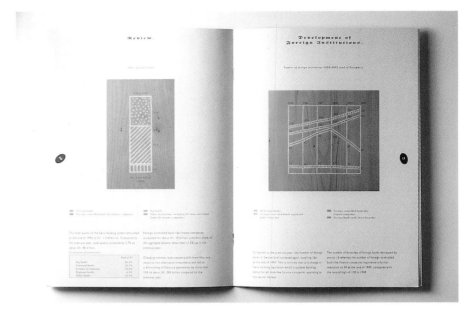

Merit/International

ANNUAL REPORT
19th Brazilian Creative Annual
ART DIRECTOR *Javier Talavera*
CREATIVE DIRECTOR *Javier Talavera*
DESIGNER *Claudia Issa*
PHOTOGRAPHERS *Arnaldo Pappalardo,
Reinaldo Coser*
PRODUCER *Fabio B. Cardoso*
AGENCY *Foote, Cone & Belding, São Paulo*
CLIENT *Clube de Criacão de São Paulo*

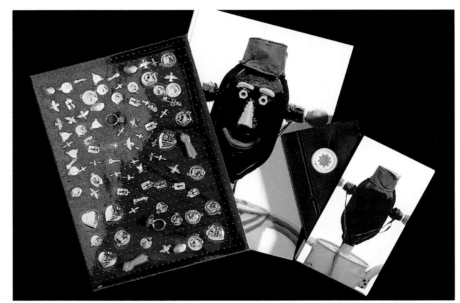

Merit/National

BOOKLET, FOLDER, OR BROCHURE, SINGLE
SYZYGY
ART DIRECTOR *Matthew L. Doty*
DESIGNER *Matthew L. Doty*
COPYWRITER *Matthew L. Doty*
PHOTOGRAPHER *Barbara Strong Doty*
ILLUSTRATOR *Matthew L. Doty*
PRODUCERS *Matthew L. Doty, Barbara Strong Doty*
ILLUSTRATOR *Lili Hertzler*
AGENCY *Strong Productions, Inc.*
CLIENT *Strong Productions, Inc.*

Merit/National

BOOKLET, FOLDER, OR BROCHURE, SINGLE
Advancing the Science of Investing
ART DIRECTOR *John Bielenberg*
CREATIVE DIRECTOR *Greg Galle*
DESIGNERS *John Bielenberg, Allen Ashton*
COPYWRITER *Maureen Oddone*
PHOTOGRAPHER *Doug Menuez*
AGENCY *Mathew Krieger & Associates*
STUDIO *Bielenberg Design*
CLIENT *Wells Fargo Nikko Investment Advisors*

Mystery Table 1993
Steel, marble, stainless steel
59 1/2 x 104 x 18 1/2

Merit/National

BOOKLET, FOLDER, OR BROCHURE, SINGLE
Albert Paley: Organic Logic
DESIGNERS *Michael Bierut, Esther Bridavsky*
PHOTOGRAPHER *Bruce Miller*
STUDIO *Pentagram Design*
CLIENT *Peter Joseph Gallery*

Merit/National

BOOKLET, FOLDER, OR BROCHURE, SINGLE
MTV Video Music Awards Program Guide
ART DIRECTORS *Stacy Drummond, Jeffrey Keyton,*
Tracy Boychuk, David Felton, Johan Vipper
ILLUSTRATORS *Various*
AGENCY *MTV Off Air Creative*
CLIENT *MTV Music Television*

Merit/National

ANNUAL REPORT
*Woodland Park Zoological Society 1993
Annual Report*
ART DIRECTOR *Dennis Clouse*
DESIGNERS *Dennis Clouse, Traci Daberko*
COPYWRITERS *Dennis Clouse, J. Pasquarelli*
PHOTOGRAPHERS *Dennis Clouse, Traci Daberko*
ILLUSTRATOR *Dennis Clouse*
STUDIO *The Leonhardt Group*
CLIENT *Woodland Park Zoological Society, Seattle*

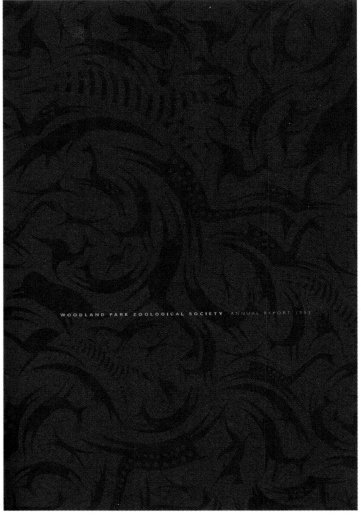

Merit/National

BOOKLET, FOLDER, OR BROCHURE, SINGLE
Redefining the Instant Image
ART DIRECTOR *Jon Craine*
CREATIVE DIRECTOR *Jon Craine*
DESIGNERS *John Rushworth, Jon Craine*
ILLUSTRATOR *Pentagram, United Kingdom*
PRODUCER *Polaroid Corporation, United Kingdom*
CLIENT *Polaroid Corporation*

Merit/National

BOOKLET, FOLDER, OR BROCHURE, SINGLE
Art Catalogue for Armory Show, November 1994
ART DIRECTOR *Kimberly Baer*
CREATIVE DIRECTOR *Kimberly Baer*
DESIGNER *Margaret van Oppen*
COPYWRITERS *Karen Moss, Carolyn Wendt*
PHOTOGRAPHER *David Familian*
STUDIO *Kimberly Baer Design Associates*
CLIENT *Pasadena Art Alliance*

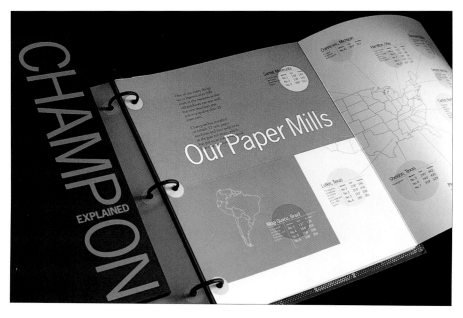

Merit/National

BOOKLET, FOLDER, OR BROCHURE, SINGLE
Encounters
DESIGNER *Catt Lyon Design*
PHOTOGRAPHER *Gregory Thorpe*
CLIENT *The Hennegan Company*

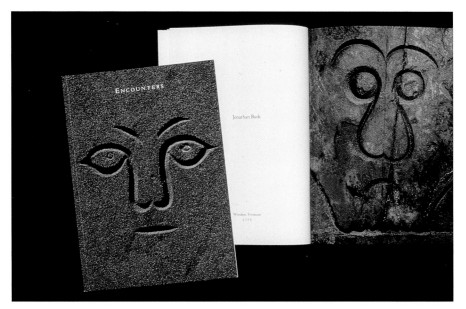

Merit/National

BOOKLET, FOLDER, OR BROCHURE, SINGLE
Champion Explained Corporate Booklet
ART DIRECTORS *Stephen Doyle, Tom Kluepfel*
DESIGNERS *Chuck Robertson, Mats Hakansson, Vanessa Eckstein, Gary Tooth*
STUDIO *Drenttel Doyle Partners*
CLIENT *Champion International Corporation*

Merit/National

BOOKLET, FOLDER, OR BROCHURE, SINGLE
The Aeron Chair by Herman Miller
ART DIRECTOR *Michael Barile*
CREATIVE DIRECTOR *Michael Barile*
DESIGNERS *Michael Barile, Yang Kim*
COPYWRITER *Debra Wierenga*
PHOTOGRAPHERS *Nick Merrick, Jim Hedrich*
ILLUSTRATOR *Gould Design*
PRINTER *Etheridge Company*
CLIENT *Herman Miller Inc.*

Merit/National

BOOKLET, FOLDER, OR BROCHURE, SINGLE
Country Music Memories
ART DIRECTOR *Marti Golon*
DIRECTOR OF DESIGN *Tom Bentkowski*
PHOTO EDITOR *Adrienne Aurichio*
PHOTOGRAPHER *Hans Neleman*
CLIENT *Life Magazine*

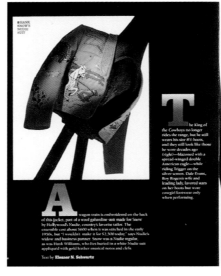

Merit/National

BOOKLET, FOLDER, OR BROCHURE, SINGLE
Ethical Culture Fieldston Schools Viewbook
ART DIRECTOR *Anthony Rutka*
DESIGNER *Priscilla Henderer*
COPYWRITER *Joan Weadock*
PHOTOGRAPHER *Mark Jenkinson*
STUDIO *Rutka Weadock Design*
CLIENT *Ethical Culture Fieldston Schools*

Merit/National

BOOKLET, FOLDER, OR BROCHURE, SINGLE
Objects: Sixteen L.A. Sculptors
ART DIRECTOR *Rebeca Méndez*
DESIGNER *Darin Beaman*
COPYWRITERS *The featured artists*
PHOTOGRAPHERS *Art Center photography students*
STUDIO *Art Center Design Office*
CLIENT *Art Center College of Design*

Merit/National

BOOKLET, FOLDER, OR BROCHURE, SINGLE
Grayhawk
ART DIRECTOR *Steve Ditko*
CREATIVE DIRECTOR *Steve Ditko*
DESIGNERS *Steve Ditko, Stacy Johansen*
COPYWRITER *Jerry Rose*
ILLUSTRATOR *John Kleber*
STUDIO *CFD Design*
CLIENT *Grayhawk Development*

Merit/National

BOOKLET, FOLDER, OR BROCHURE, SINGLE
Herman Miller for the Home Binder
ART DIRECTOR *Michael Barile*
CREATIVE DIRECTOR *Michael Barile*
DESIGNERS *Michael Barile, Yang Kim, Adam Smith,
Glenn Hoffman*
COPYWRITER *Dick Holm*
PHOTOGRAPHY *Phil Schaafsma,
Herman Miller Archives*
PRINTER *Burch Inc.*
CLIENT *Herman Miller Inc.*

Merit/National

BOOKLET, FOLDER, OR BROCHURE, SINGLE
Motorola It Doesn't Take a Genius Kit
ART DIRECTOR *James Carlton*
CREATIVE DIRECTOR *James Carlton*
DESIGNERS *Krista Ferdinand, Victoria Huang*
COPYWRITER *Brian Agne*
ILLUSTRATOR *Richard Goldberg*
STUDIO *Design Horizons International*
CLIENT *Motorola*

Merit/National

BOOKLET, FOLDER, OR BROCHURE, SINGLE
Brochure
ART DIRECTOR *Nora Vaivads*
CREATIVE DIRECTOR *Gary Goldsmith*
DESIGNER *Nora Vaivads*
COPYWRITER *Justin Rohrlich*
PHOTOGRAPHY *Stock*
STUDIO *Goldsmith/Jeffrey*
CLIENT *CondoExchange*

Merit/National

BOOKLET, FOLDER, OR BROCHURE, SINGLE
1995 Consumer Catalogue
ART DIRECTOR *David Covell*
CREATIVE DIRECTOR *Michael Jager*
DESIGNERS *David Covell, Ian Factor, Dan Sharp,*
Jim Anfuso, Mark Sylvester, John Phemister
COPYWRITER *David Shriber*
STUDIO *Jager Di Paola Kemp Design*
CLIENT *Burton Snowboards*

Merit/National

BOOKLET, FOLDER, OR BROCHURE, SINGLE
Hush Puppies Riverbuck Brochure
ART DIRECTOR *Jaimie Alexander*
DESIGNER *Paul Westrick*
COPYWRITER *Sarah Spatt*
PHOTOGRAPHER *Mark Steele*
STUDIO *Fitch Inc.*
CLIENT *Hush Puppies Company*

Merit/National

BOOKLET, FOLDER, OR BROCHURE, SINGLE
Buttered Side Up Brochure
ART DIRECTOR *David Lerch*
DESIGNER *David Lerch*
COPYWRITERS *Bernard Brunon, Edward Albee,*
Mary Ross Taylor
PHOTOGRAPHER *Thomas A. DuBrock*
STUDIO *Geer Design, Inc.*
CLIENT *Lawndale Art and Performance Center*

Merit/National

BOOKLET, FOLDER, OR BROCHURE, SINGLE
1995 Dealer Catalogue
ART DIRECTOR *David Covell*
CREATIVE DIRECTOR *Michael Jager*
DESIGNERS *David Covell, Ian Factor, Dan Sharp,*
Keith Brown
COPYWRITER *David Shriber*
STUDIO *Jager Di Paola Kemp Design*
CLIENT *Burton Snowboards*

Merit/National

BOOKLET, FOLDER, OR BROCHURE, SINGLE
*Connections 2: Explorations in the Getty Center
Collections Brochure*
DESIGNER *Mike Fink*
STUDIO *J. Paul Getty Trust, Publication Services*
CLIENT *The Getty Center for the History of Art and
the Humanities*

Merit/National

BOOKLET, FOLDER, OR BROCHURE, SINGLE
Kivar Performa for DSI
ART DIRECTOR *Mickey Boisvert*
DESIGNER *Mickey Boisvert*
COPYWRITER *Susan G. Mattei*
PHOTOGRAPHER *Adam Laipson*
CLIENT *Decorative Specialties International Inc.*

Merit/National

BOOKLET, FOLDER, OR BROCHURE, SINGLE
Separating Black and White Photography
ART DIRECTOR *Tom Geismar*
DESIGNER *Cathy Schaefer*
PHOTOGRAPHER *David Arky*
STUDIO *Chermayeff & Geismar*
CLIENT *Monadnock Paper Mills, Inc.*

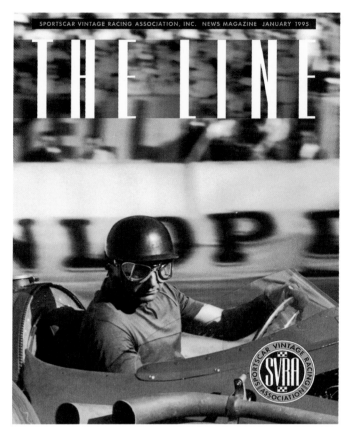

SPORTSCAR VINTAGE RACING ASSOCIATION, INC. NEWS MAGAZINE JANUARY 1995

THE LINE

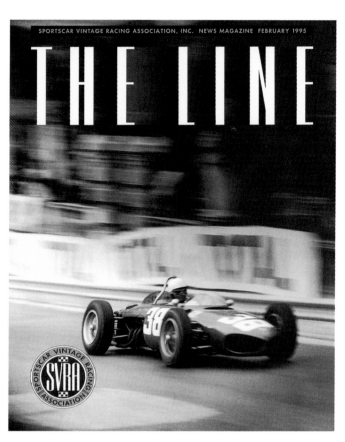

SPORTSCAR VINTAGE RACING ASSOCIATION, INC. NEWS MAGAZINE FEBRUARY 1995

THE LINE

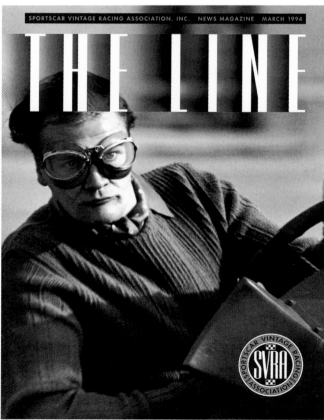

SPORTSCAR VINTAGE RACING ASSOCIATION, INC. NEWS MAGAZINE MARCH 1994

THE LINE

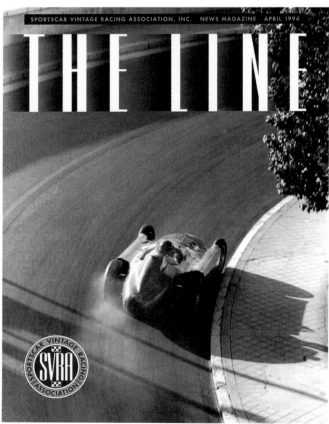

SPORTSCAR VINTAGE RACING ASSOCIATION, INC. NEWS MAGAZINE APRIL 1994

THE LINE

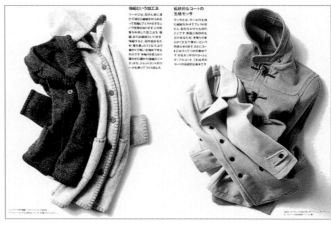

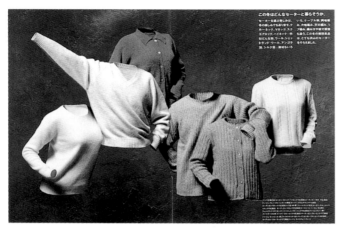

Merit/International

BOOKLET, FOLDER, OR BROCHURE, SERIES
Mujirushi-Ryohin Clothing Catalogue, Winter 1994
ART DIRECTOR *Masaaki Hiromura*
BRAND DIRECTORS *Ikko Tanaka, Kazuko Koike*
DESIGNERS *Masaaki Hiromura, Toshiyuki Kojima*
COPYWRITER *Yoichi Umemoto*
PHOTOGRAPHER *Takashi Oyama*
ILLUSTRATOR *Kazuya Takeuchi*
CLIENT *Ryohin-Keikaku Co., Ltd.*

Merit/International

BOOKLET, FOLDER, OR BROCHURE, SERIES
Bally Magalogues
ART DIRECTOR *Antonie Reinhard*
CREATIVE DIRECTOR *Antonie Reinhard*
DESIGNER *Martin Gaberthüel*
COPYWRITER *Margrit Brunswick*
PHOTOGRAPHER *Hanspeter Schneider*
AGENCY *Seiler DDB Needham AG Bern*
CLIENT *Bally International AG*

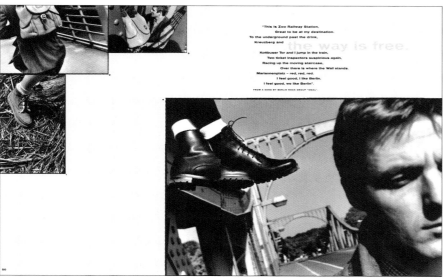

BOOKLET, FOLDER, OR BROCHURE, SERIES
Butterfield & Robinson Winter Trips
ART DIRECTOR *Frank Viva*
CREATIVE DIRECTORS *Frank Viva, Doug Dolan*
DESIGNER *Frank Viva*
COPYWRITER *Doug Dolan*
ILLUSTRATORS *Frank Viva, Karen Satok*
STUDIO *Viva Dolan Communications & Design*
CLIENT *Butterfield & Robinson*

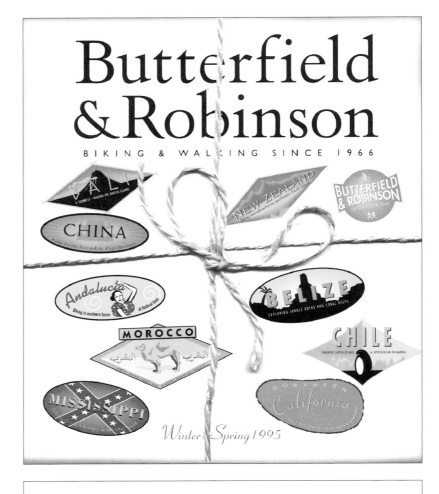

BOOKLET, FOLDER, OR BROCHURE, SERIES
Butterfield & Robinson Homes Away
ART DIRECTOR *Frank Viva*
CREATIVE DIRECTORS *Frank Viva, Doug Dolan*
DESIGNER *Karen Satok*
COPYWRITER *Doug Dolan*
STUDIO *Viva Dolan Communications & Design*
CLIENT *Butterfield & Robinson*

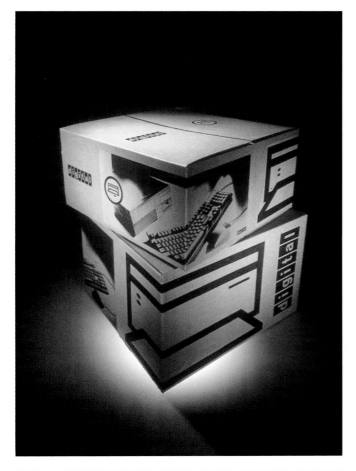

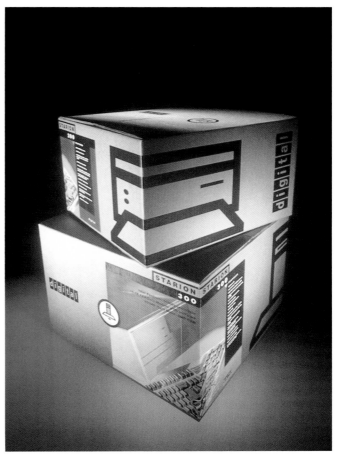

Merit/National

PACKAGING, SERIES
DEC PC Packaging System
ART DIRECTORS *Robert Wood, Tammie Hunt*
CREATIVE DIRECTOR *Robert Wood*
PHOTOGRAPHER *Peter Medilik*
STUDIO *Fitch Inc.*
CLIENT *Digital Equipment Corporation*

Merit/International

PACKAGING, SERIES
Boots Laundry
ART DIRECTOR *Mary Lewis*
DESIGNERS *Kasia Rust, Mary Lewis*
STUDIO *Lewis Moberly*
CLIENT *The Boots Company Plc*

Merit/International

PACKAGING, SERIES
Circus Sugar
ART DIRECTOR *Frauke Dirksen*
CREATIVE DIRECTOR *Ralph Taubenberger*
COPYWRITER *Axel Simon*
ILLUSTRATOR *Frauke Dirksen*
AGENCY *Heye + Partner*
CLIENT *Südzucker AG*

Merit/International

PACKAGING, SERIES
Hats of the World Sugar
ART DIRECTOR *Frauke Dirksen*
CREATIVE DIRECTOR *Ralph Taubenberger*
COPYWRITER *Axel Simon*
ILLUSTRATOR *Frauke Dirksen*
AGENCY *Heye + Partner*
CLIENT *Südzucker AG*

Merit/International

PACKAGING, SERIES
UCC Black Coffee 900 ml
ART DIRECTOR *Takaaki Goto*
CREATIVE DIRECTOR *Jyushiro Miura*
DESIGNER *Takaaki Goto*
CLIENT *UCC Ueshima Coffee Co., Ltd.*

Merit/National

ANNOUNCEMENT, INVITATION, OR MENU, SINGLE
Maisel Birth Announcement
CREATIVE DIRECTOR *Richard Anwyl*
DESIGNER *Karen Betz*
COPYWRITER *Richard Anwyl*
PHOTOGRAPHER *Jay Maisel*
CLIENT *Jay and L. A. Maisel*

Merit/National

ANNOUNCEMENT, INVITATION, OR MENU, SINGLE
Matthew Spitzley's Birth Announcement
ART DIRECTOR *John Ball*
PHOTO ART DIRECTOR *Jose Serrano*
DESIGNER *John Ball*
PHOTOGRAPHER *Carl VanderSchuit*
AGENCY *Mires Design, Inc.*
STUDIO *Mires Design, Inc.*
CLIENT *Gale and John Spitzley*

Merit/National

ANNOUNCEMENT, INVITATION, OR MENU, SINGLE
MTV Video Music Awards Invitation
ART DIRECTOR *Christopher Davis*
CREATIVE DIRECTOR *Jeffrey Keyton*
DESIGNER *Christopher Davis*
COPYWRITER *David Lanfair*
PHOTOGRAPHER *Christopher Davis*
AGENCY *MTV Off Air Creative*
CLIENT *MTV Music Television*

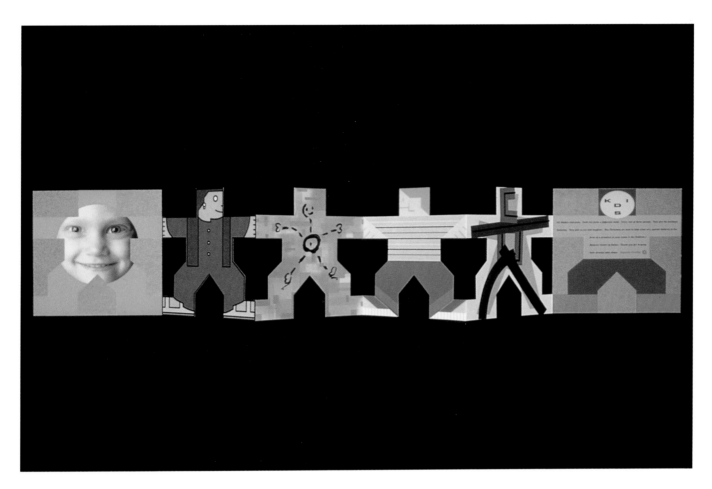

Merit/National

ANNOUNCEMENT, INVITATION, OR MENU, SINGLE
Holiday Shapes Christmas Card
ART DIRECTOR *Chuck Johnson*
CREATIVE DIRECTOR *Chuck Johnson*
DESIGNER *Chuck Johnson*
COPYWRITER *Chuck Johnson*
PHOTOGRAPHER *Will Crocker*
ILLUSTRATORS *Bryan Flynn, Rob Smith,*
Chuck Johnson, Ken Koester
STUDIO *Brainstorm, Inc.*
CLIENT *Yaquinto Printing*

Merit/National

ANNOUNCEMENT, INVITATION, OR MENU, SINGLE
*Cine City: Film and Perceptions of Urban
Space 1895—1995 Brochure*
DESIGNER *David Mellen*
STUDIO *J. Paul Getty Trust, Publication Services*
CLIENT *The Getty Center for the History of Art and
the Humanities*

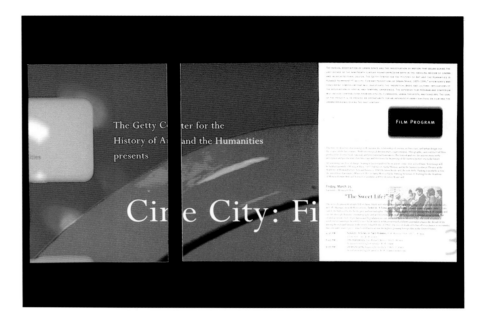

Merit/National

ANNOUNCEMENT, INVITATION, OR MENU, SINGLE
*Connections 2: Explorations in the Getty Center
Collections Announcement*
DESIGNER *Mike Fink*
STUDIO *J. Paul Getty Trust, Publication Services*
CLIENT *The Getty Center for the History of Art and
the Humanities*

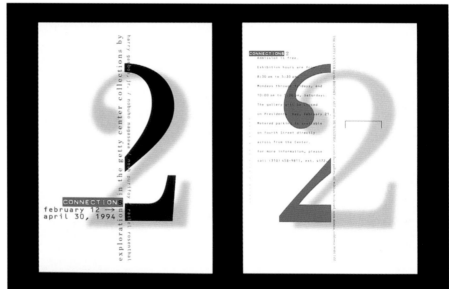

Merit/National

ANNOUNCEMENT, INVITATION, OR MENU, SINGLE
SHR Perceptual Management Christmas Card
ART DIRECTOR *Barry Shepard*
DESIGNER *Nathan Joseph*
COPYWRITER *Nathan Joseph*
AGENCY *SHR Perceptual Management*
CLIENT *SHR Perceptual Management*

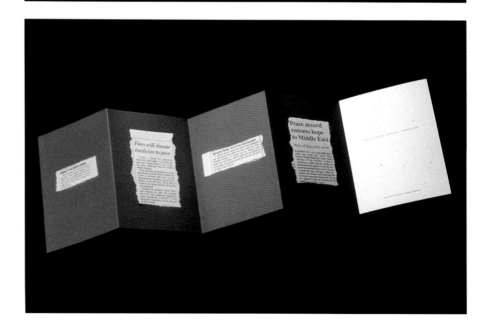

Merit/National

LETTERHEAD, BUSINESS CARD, ENVELOPE
The Stone Kitchen Stationery
ART DIRECTOR *Mark Geer*
DESIGNER *Mark Geer*
PHOTOGRAPHER *Key Sanders*
ILLUSTRATOR *Mark Geer*
STUDIO *Geer Design, Inc.*
CLIENT *The Stone Kitchen*

Merit/National

LETTERHEAD, BUSINESS CARD, ENVELOPE
ACME Stationery Package
ART DIRECTOR *Dave Eliason*
CREATIVE DIRECTOR *Bryan L. Peterson*
DESIGNER *Dave Eliason*
AGENCY *Peterson & Company*
STUDIO *Peterson & Company*
CLIENT *ACME Rubber Stamp Co.*

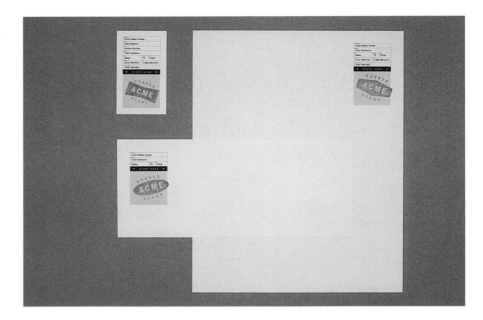

Merit/National

LETTERHEAD, BUSINESS CARD, ENVELOPE
Linda J. Holland Stationery
ART DIRECTOR *Rick Baptist*
DESIGNER *Rick Baptist*
ILLUSTRATOR *Rick Baptist*
AGENCY *FGI*
CLIENT *Linda J. Holland*

Merit/International

LETTERHEAD, BUSINESS CARD, ENVELOPE
Dialog Letterhead, Comp Slip, Business Card,
Report Cover
ART DIRECTOR *Peter Smith*
CREATIVE DIRECTOR *Peter Smith*
DESIGNER *André Soukias*
CLIENT *Dialog Limited*

Merit/National

PUBLIC SERVICE, SINGLE
Cleveland Institute of Art Catalogue 1994–95
ART DIRECTORS *Joyce Nesnadny, Mark Schwartz*
CREATIVE DIRECTORS *Joyce Nesnadny,*
Mark Schwartz
DESIGNERS *Joyce Nesnadny, Brian Lavy*
COPYWRITER *Anne Brooks Ranallo*
PHOTOGRAPHERS *Robert Muller, Mark Schwartz*
AGENCY *Nesnadny + Schwartz*
STUDIO *Nesnadny + Schwartz*
CLIENT *Cleveland Institute of Art*

Merit/National

PUBLIC SERVICE, SINGLE
Box
ART DIRECTOR *Wendy Hansen*
CREATIVE DIRECTOR *Lyle Wedemeyer*
DESIGNER *Wendy Hansen*
COPYWRITER *Chris Preston*
PRODUCER *Renee Kirsch*
AGENCY *Martin/Williams*
CLIENT *Salvation Army*

Merit/National

PUBLIC SERVICE, SINGLE
Stay in School Bus Poster
ART DIRECTOR *Stephen Doyle*
DESIGNER *Gary Tooth*
PHOTOGRAPHER *William Wegman*
STUDIO *Drenttel Doyle Partners*
CLIENT *TDI*

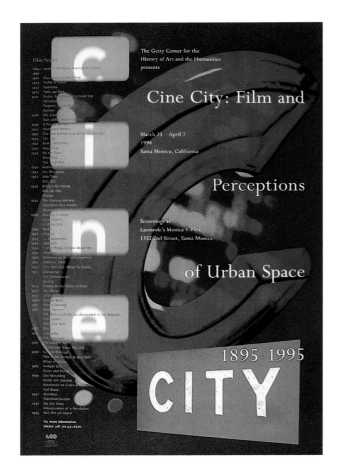

Merit/National

POSTER, OTHER THAN ADVERTISING, SINGLE
Cine City: Film and Perceptions of Urban Space
1895–1995
DESIGNER *David Mellen*
STUDIO *J. Paul Getty Trust, Publication Services*
CLIENT *The Getty Center for the History of Art and the Humanities*

Merit/National

POSTER, OTHER THAN ADVERTISING, SINGLE
Bay Street Bird
ART DIRECTOR *Paul Davis*
DESIGNER *Paul Davis*
ILLUSTRATOR *Paul Davis*
STUDIO *Paul Davis Studio*
CLIENT *Bay Street Theatre Festival 1994*

Merit/National

POSTER, OTHER THAN ADVERTISING, SINGLE
Human Rights Watch 1994
ART DIRECTOR *Paul Davis*
DESIGNER *Paul Davis*
ILLUSTRATOR *Paul Davis*
STUDIO *Paul Davis Studio*
CLIENT *Human Rights Watch Film Festival*

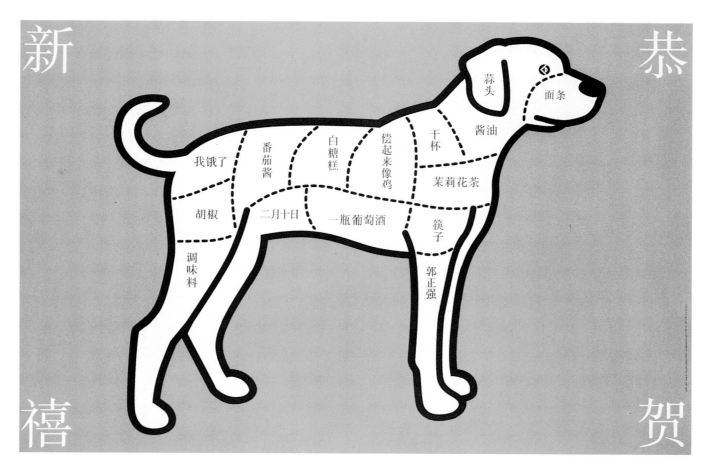

Merit/National

POSTER, OTHER THAN ADVERTISING, SINGLE
Happy New Year
ART DIRECTOR *Sam Kuo*
DESIGNER *Sam Kuo*
COPYWRITER *Sam Kuo*
ILLUSTRATOR *Sam Kuo*
STUDIO *Kuo Design Group*
CLIENT *Kuo Design Group*

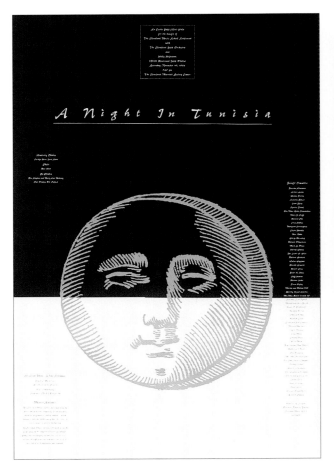

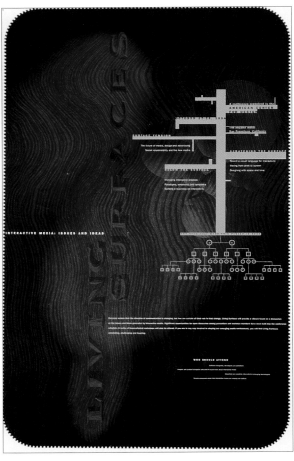

Merit/National

POSTER, OTHER THAN ADVERTISING, SINGLE
A Night in Tunisia
ART DIRECTOR *Gregory Oznowich*
DESIGNER *Gregory Oznowich*
COPYWRITER *Beatrice Kay Wyse*
ILLUSTRATIONS *Clip art*
AGENCY *Watt, Roop & Co.*
CLIENT *The Cleveland Music School Settlement*

Merit/National

POSTER, OTHER THAN ADVERTISING, SINGLE
Living Surfaces
ART DIRECTOR *Anthony Ma*
DESIGNER *Anthony Ma*
COPYWRITERS *Paul Souza, Rob Dewey*
ILLUSTRATOR *Grant Davis*
STUDIO *Tanagram*
CLIENT *American Center for Design*

Merit/National

POSTER, OTHER THAN ADVERTISING, SINGLE
Risk
ART DIRECTOR *Stephen Doyle*
DESIGNERS *Gary Tooth, Stephen Doyle*
STUDIO *Drenttel Doyle Partners*
CLIENT *Type Directors Club*

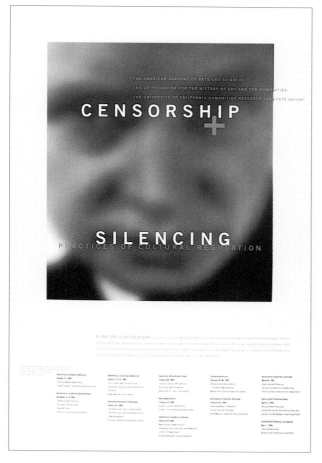

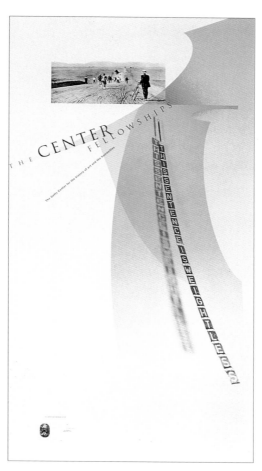

Merit/National

POSTER, OTHER THAN ADVERTISING, SINGLE
Censorship and Silencing: Practices of Cultural Regulation
DESIGNERS *Sean Adams, Noreen Morioka*
STUDIO *J. Paul Getty Trust, Publication Services*
CLIENT *The Getty Center for the History of Art and the Humanities*

Merit/National

POSTER, OTHER THAN ADVERTISING, SINGLE
The Getty Center for the History of Art and the Humanities
ART DIRECTOR *Rebeca Méndez*
CREATIVE DIRECTOR *Rebeca Méndez*
DESIGNER *Rebeca Méndez*
PHOTOGRAPHERS *John Kiffe, Jobe Benjan*
ARTWORK *George Brotch*
CLIENT *The Getty Center for the History of Art and the Humanities*

Merit/National

POSTER, OTHER THAN ADVERTISING, SINGLE
Wolf Teaser
ART DIRECTOR *Kim Wexman*
CREATIVE DIRECTOR *Peter Bemis*
COPYWRITER *Ari Sherman*
PHOTOGRAPHER *Michael O'Neil*
AGENCY *Frankfurt Balkind Partners*
CLIENT *Columbia Pictures*

Merit/National

POSTER, OTHER THAN ADVERTISING, SINGLE
AIGA Communication Graphics Call for Entries
ART DIRECTOR *Woody Pirtle*
DESIGNERS *Woody Pirtle, Ivette Montes de Oca*
ILLUSTRATOR *Woody Pirtle*
STUDIO *Pentagram Design*
CLIENT *AIGA*

Merit/National

POSTER, OTHER THAN ADVERTISING, SINGLE
Richard III
ART DIRECTOR *James Victore*
DESIGNER *James Victore*
PRODUCER *Julie Sheehan*
DIRECTOR *Scott Cargle*
STUDIO *Victore Design Works*
CLIENT *The Shakespeare Project*

Merit/National

POSTER, OTHER THAN ADVERTISING, SINGLE
Twelfth Night
ART DIRECTOR *James Victore*
DESIGNER *James Victore*
PRODUCER *Julie Sheehan*
DIRECTOR *Scott Cargle*
STUDIO *Victore Design Works*
CLIENT *The Shakespeare Project*

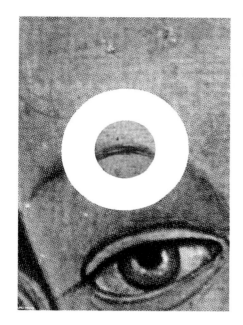

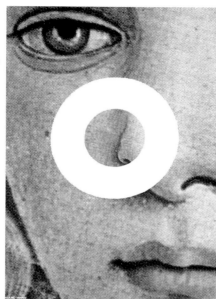

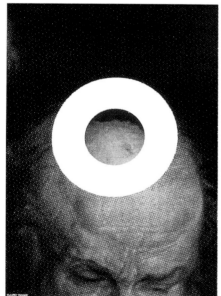

Merit/International

POSTER, OTHER THAN ADVERTISING, SERIES
One's Point of View
ART DIRECTOR *Kijuro Yahagi*
DESIGNER *Kijuro Yahagi*

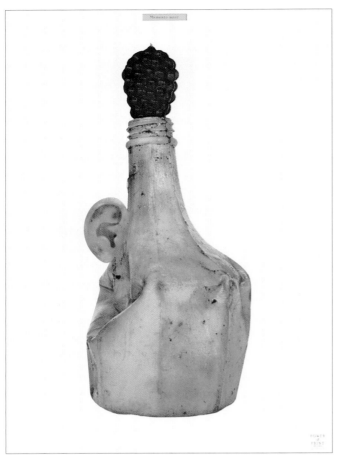

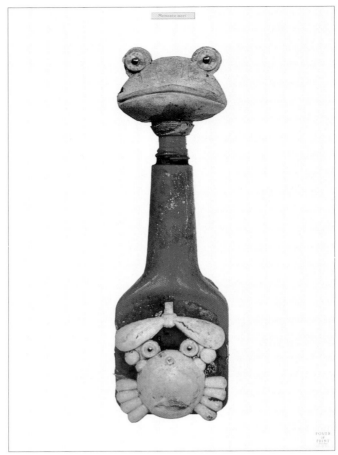

(facing page)
Merit/International

POSTER, OTHER THAN ADVERTISING, SERIES
Memento Mori
ART DIRECTOR *Shotaro Sakaguchi*
DESIGNER *Shotaro Sakaguchi*
PHOTOGRAPHER *Shotaro Sakaguchi*
AGENCY *Dentsu, Inc.*
STUDIO *Dentsu Cotec Inc.*
CLIENT *Dentsu Cotec Inc.*

(above)
Merit/National

SELF-PROMOTION, SINGLE
Parallel T-Shirts
ART DIRECTORS *Neil Powell, Alan Leusink*
CREATIVE DIRECTOR *Joe Duffy*
DESIGNERS *Neil Powell, Alan Leusink*
ILLUSTRATORS *Neil Powell, Alan Leusink*
STUDIO *Duffy Design*
CLIENT *Parallel Productions*

This is what happens when a client fires an agency.

Coming from an advertising agency, what we are about to suggest may surprise you.

It has been our experience that the single best way for a client to build his business is to fire his agency.

We are referring not to the firings that wash in on the morning tide of the daily ad columns. The kind of firing we are talking about is far more difficult.

But potentially more rewarding.

Namely, the ability to breathe life and spirit into an advertising idea; the talent to ignite, inflame, inspire; to fill an agency with passion, excitement and enthusiasm.

We've been very lucky. We have clients that fire us on a daily basis. Clients who question. Clients who push. Clients who challenge preconceived notions of how advertising should look, feel and sound. Clients who are comfortable with the fact that good ideas will make them uncomfortable.

Fire your agency and you will find its people will work harder for you; will play over their heads; will do groundbreaking work. When this happens, the result is advertising that not only wins sales for a client. But critical acclaim.

Take the recent International Advertising Festival at Cannes, the industry's most prestigious competition. Better yet, take the past three years of Cannes.

For an unprecedented three years in a row, DDB Needham won more Lions than any other agency in the world.

This year we took home 21 Lions. For 15 clients from 7 countries.

For clients with big budgets. Clients with small budgets. And clients with no budgets.

Clients from all corners of the world with marketing challenges as different as the languages they speak. Yet with one thing in common. They view advertising not as art. Not as science. But as business.

They are totally committed to inspiring creativity because they understand and value its power. And have seen firsthand just how big a contribution it can make to their business.

They've come to the realization that in a world of product parity, great advertising is very often the marketing difference.

Don't get us wrong. We aren't shifting the onus of doing great work onto our clients. But they do share the responsibility. The simple fact is that great clients make great agencies. It doesn't work the other way around.

Or put another way, even the best ideas an agency has are only dry kindling without the spark that comes from the client.

So, now you know what happens when a client fires an agency. But that's only half the story. You should hear what happens when an agency fires a client.

Call me, Keith Reinhard, at 212-415-3028.

Merit/National

SELF-PROMOTION, SINGLE
*This Is What Happens When a Client Fires
an Agency*
ART DIRECTOR *John Staffen*
CREATIVE DIRECTORS *Mike Rogers, John Staffen*
COPYWRITER *Mike Rogers*
AGENCY *DDB Needham Worldwide/New York*
CLIENT *DDB Needham Worldwide/New York*

Merit/National

SELF-PROMOTION, SINGLE
Louise Fili Ltd. Promotion
ART DIRECTOR *Louise Fili*
CREATIVE DIRECTOR *Louise Fili*
DESIGNERS *Louise Fili, Leah Lococo*
COPYWRITER *Steven Heller*
PHOTOGRAPHERS *Ed Spiro, David Barry*
STUDIO *Louise Fili Ltd.*
CLIENT *Louise Fili Ltd.*

Merit/National

SELF-PROMOTION, SINGLE
Pleasure Place Mailer
ART DIRECTOR *Morton Jackson*
CREATIVE DIRECTOR *Morton Jackson*
DESIGNER *Morton Jackson*
PHOTOGRAPHER *Martin Schulman*
STUDIO *Graffito*
CLIENT *Pleasure Place*

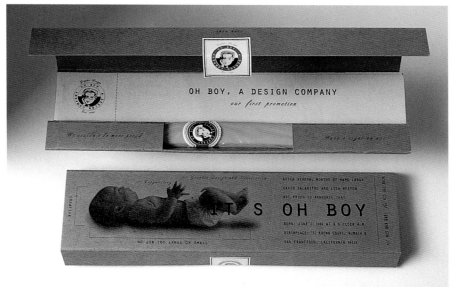

Merit/National

SELF-PROMOTION, SINGLE
Birth Announcement
ART DIRECTOR *David Salanitro*
DESIGNER *David Salanitro*
COPYWRITER *David Salanitro*
STUDIO *Oh Boy, A Design Company*
CLIENT *Oh Boy, A Design Company*

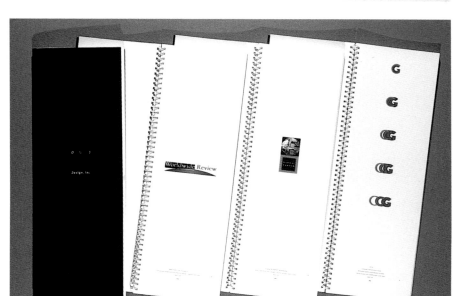

Merit/National

SELF-PROMOTION, SINGLE
Identities by O & J Design, Inc.
ART DIRECTOR *Andrzej J. Olejniczak*
DESIGNERS *Andrzej J. Olejniczak,*
Andrew Jablonski, Inhi Clara Kim,
Lia Camara-Mariscal
COPYWRITER *Nancy L. Baxter*
CLIENT *O & J Design, Inc.*

Merit/National

SELF-PROMOTION, SINGLE
No. IX, Toy Box
ART DIRECTOR *Janet Kruse*
DESIGNERS *Janet Kruse, Traci Daberko*
PHOTOGRAPHERS *Bill Cannon, Marco Prozzo*
ILLUSTRATORS *Various*
PRODUCER *Dan Snyder*
CLIENT *Pat Hackett, Artist Representative*

Merit/National

SELF-PROMOTION, SINGLE
How Good Is Your Taste?
ART DIRECTOR *Michael Gericke*
DESIGNERS *Michael Gericke, Ed Chiquitucto*
COPYWRITER *Frederick Shamlian*
ILLUSTRATOR *Pentagram Design*
STUDIO *Pentagram Design*
CLIENT *Pentagram Design*

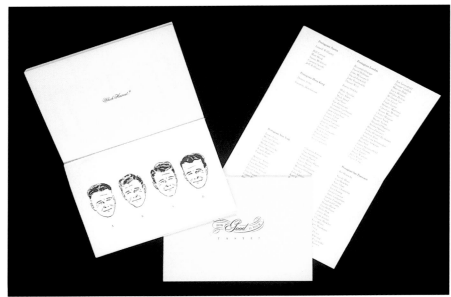

Merit/National

SELF-PROMOTION, SINGLE
Pushpin Jr.
ART DIRECTOR *Seymour Chwast*
CREATIVE DIRECTOR *Seymour Chwast*
DESIGNER *Roxanne Slimak*
COPYWRITER *Seymour Chwast*
STUDIO *The Pushpin Group, Inc.*
CLIENT *The Pushpin Group, Inc.*

Merit/National

SELF-PROMOTION, SINGLE
Agency Print Piece
ART DIRECTOR *Grant Richards*
CREATIVE DIRECTORS *Todd Tilford, Grant Richards*
COPYWRITER *Todd Tilford*
PRODUCER *Gail Beckman*
AGENCY *The Richards Group*
CLIENT *The Richards Group*

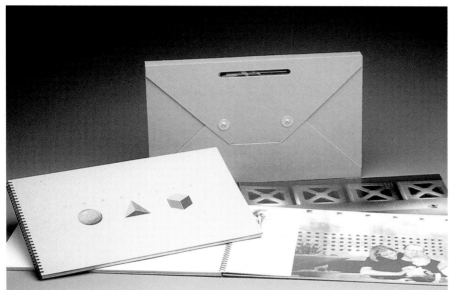

Merit/National

SELF-PROMOTION, SINGLE
Set Design Promotion
ART DIRECTORS *Gary M. Hill, Bill Tonnesen*
CREATIVE DIRECTOR *Bill Tonnesen*
DESIGNER *Gary M. Hill*
COPYWRITER *Bill Tonnesen*
AGENCY *Dunn & Hill*
CLIENT *Tonnesen Sets*

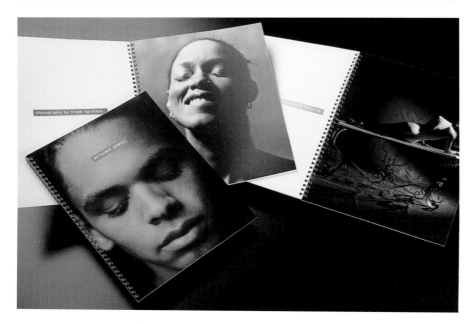

Merit/National

SELF-PROMOTION, SINGLE
Marchese Brochure
ART DIRECTOR *Don Carter*
DESIGNER *Don Carter*
COPYWRITER *Don Carter*
PHOTOGRAPHER *Frank Marchese*
PRODUCER *Susan Bunn*
AGENCY *Mintz & Hoke*
CLIENT *Frank Marchese*

Merit/National

SELF-PROMOTION, SINGLE
TV Dinner
ART DIRECTOR *Douglass Grimmett*
DESIGNER *Douglass Grimmett*
COPYWRITER *Douglass Grimmett*
ILLUSTRATOR *Douglass Grimmett*
CLIENT *Douglass Grimmett*

Merit/International

SELF-PROMOTION, SINGLE
A Bag of Batey Culture
ART DIRECTOR *Eddie Wong*
CREATIVE DIRECTOR *Jim Aitchison*
DESIGNER *Eddie Wong*
COPYWRITERS *Ian Batey, Sim Yang Seah,*
Jim Aitchison
ILLUSTRATIONS *Eddie Wong and stock*
AGENCY *Batey Ads Singapore*
CLIENT *Batey Ads Singapore*

Merit/National

SELF-PROMOTION, SERIES
Champion Carnival Text and Cover Sourcebooks
ART DIRECTOR *Bart Crosby*
CREATIVE DIRECTOR *Bart Crosby*
DESIGNER *Angela Norwood*
PHOTOGRAPHER *Laurie Rubin*
STUDIO *Crosby Associates Inc.*
CLIENT *Champion International Corporation*

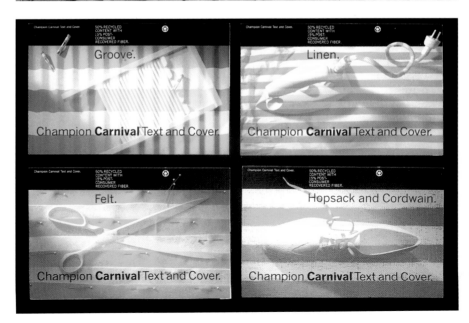

Gold Medalist/National

FULL PAGE OR SPREAD
Henry Rollins
CREATIVE DIRECTOR *Fred Woodward*
PHOTO EDITOR *Jodi Peckman*
PHOTOGRAPHER *Matt Mahurin*
CLIENT *Rolling Stone*

HIDDEN IN THE FOLDS

THE LANGUOR OF DRAPERY
IN THE CLASSICAL MODE

Velvet-and-metal collar, above, by Anat Greinesky, about $350.
At Anat Greinesky, 38 rue Sedaine, Paris. Bronze chiffon coat, Bill Blass, $1,550.
At Saks Fifth Avenue. Right: Rayon dress, about $705, and peplum, about $715,
both by Comme des Garçons. At Barneys New York.

PHOTOGRAPHS BY SARAH MOON

Chiffon dress with draped back, above, by Donna Karan. To order, through Bergdorf Goodman.
Left: Strapless moucadrine dress, Bill Blass, $4,690. At Saks Fifth Avenue

PHOTOGRAPHS BY SARAH MOON FOR THE NEW YORK TIMES

Rayon-and-cotton bolero, above, by Comme des Garçons, about $1,275. At Barneys New York.
Right: Layered silk chiffon bias dress, Robert Danes, $1,890. At Bergdorf Goodman.

Silver Medalist/National

SERIES
Hidden in the Folds
ART DIRECTOR *Janet Froelich*
DESIGNER *Cathy Gilmore-Barnes*
PHOTOGRAPHER *Sarah Moon*
CLIENT *The New York Times Magazine*

The Twilight of the Texas Rangers

For 170 years, the legendary lawmen have
faced down cattle rustlers, serial killers, and every
threat imaginable. Now they must grapple
with their most dangerous foe: the modern world.

BY ROBERT DRAPER

The end of a long ride: Retired Ranger Joaquin Jackson of Alpine.

Silver Medalist/National

SERIES
The Twilight of the Texas Rangers
ART DIRECTOR *D. J. Stout*
DESIGNERS *D. J. Stout, Nancy McMillan*
COPYWRITER *Robert Draper*
PHOTOGRAPHER *Dan Winters*
CLIENT *Texas Monthly*

IN THE SUMMER OF 1993, JOAQUIN JACKSON, THE senior member of the Texas Rangers, drove from his outpost in Alpine to the Austin headquarters, where he informed his superiors that he was hanging up his spurs. Assistant commander Bruce Casteel was visibly upset by the news. "Joaquin, you're not ready to quit," he protested. "You need to stay."

Jackson shook his head. "I just can't do it," he said. Everyone present knew what Jackson meant. Though he had been a Ranger for the past 27 years, the strapping six-foot-five lawman was only 57 and had several good years left. The murderers and drug smugglers, he could handle just as capably as always. What Joaquin Jackson could not handle were the changes taking place within his beloved Texas Rangers. "Well," said one of the secretaries after a long silence, "I guess this is the end of one era and the start of another."

In fact, the new era had already begun, and it had made Jackson sick to his stomach. Forty Department of Public Safety employees had recently made finalists for nine new Ranger positions. Five of the forty applicants were women. Friends within the DPS had told Jackson that two of the nine jobs were going to be filled by women, no matter what. Since no woman had ever been named a Ranger before, this information came as a shock to Jackson. As veteran lawmen went, Jackson had a reputation for open-mindedness. He had vocally encouraged the 1973 hiring of the Rangers' first Hispanic officer in more than fifty years. He believed that any good law enforcement agency had to adapt with the times and was hopeful that by the year **Glenn Elliott of Longview (opposite) quit the Rangers in 1987. Below: A Ranger's boots may display his distinctive badge.**

2000, Rangers would be computer experts who primarily tangled with white-collar criminals. Now, women Rangers—that was something else again. Jackson knew a few excellent female FBI agents and always thought that a woman's intuitive powers were useful investigative tools. But a Ranger had to be more than an investigator. A Ranger had to live off the land, had to withstand days of sleepless pursuit, had to fight back mobs and overpower psychopathic murderers. That was what a Ranger did. That was what Joaquin Jackson had done for the past 27 years. Could a woman do all that? Jackson was skeptical, but he wanted to see who the DPS would come up with.

When Jackson found out, he was infuriated. Cheryl Steadman was promoted from a clerical job that involved processing warrants. The other newly appointed female Ranger, Marrie Garcia, had spent the past several years in San Antonio's driver's license service. Like Steadman, Garcia had never worked a criminal case in her life. Neither Jackson nor any of the other Rangers he talked to could remember a Ranger being plucked from the ranks of the driver's license service.

This was hardly a trivial matter. After all, the elite force of 87 Texas officers has a hand in the state's biggest criminal cases, from the crime-scene investigation of the Branch Davidian compound to the pursuit of mass murderers, serial rapists, and drug lords. Arguably, Steadman and Garcia were two of the least qualified recruits in the Rangers' 170-year history. And, Jackson thought bitterly, that was obviously beside the point. DPS director Jim Wilson and Ranger chief Maurice Cook had turned their backs on tradition and responded to the political lash. So a new era was dawning, all right, and the men of Jackson's era wanted no part of it. "When they hired those

two women, that clinched it for me," Jackson says today. Another Ranger, with 18 years on the force, turned in his badge as well, citing the women as his reason. A third veteran, after putting an end to his 25 years of service, was heard to say, "Well, I'm the last rat getting off this sinking ship."

Even so, the veterans left quietly, their disenchantment with the brotherhood surmounted only by their aversion to airing dirty Ranger laundry. The hiring of the women Rangers was seen as a quirky sign of progress by the media, which did not bother to investigate whether these particular women possessed even the most rudimentary qualifications for the job. When reporters asked Marrie Garcia's father if she was up to the challenge, he declared, "Watch her shoot," as if Rangers were ever known for their marksmanship. For her part, Cheryl Steadman told the media how she placated the DPS interviewers by saying, "A good female Ranger will wear whatever she's told," as if Rangers were ever known for conformity. But then again, this was the new era.

To Joaquin Jackson and his peers, the quota-hiring of women Rangers suggests a kind of political emasculation, one that makes a mockery of the legendary law enforcement corps. To critics of the Rangers, the event was twenty years behind schedule, further proof that the state's most sanctimonious good old boys could not be trusted to march in step with the modern world.

Certainly it is true that the recent history of the Texas Rangers is the history of an organization at odds with the changing times. In a sense, however, the Rangers have always been in sync with Texas—or rather, with the part of Texas that, for better and for worse, distinguishes Texans from the rest of

Despite an exemplary record, Hispanic Ranger Rey Martinez of New Braunfels (above and opposite) was never promoted. the world. No other state boasts an equivalent to the Rangers, and in no other state would the Rangers survive its many controversies. The question, Are the Rangers necessary? involves matters so deeply embedded in the Texas psyche that it is almost never addressed. For that matter, America as a whole is entranced by this indigenous lawman; hence the recently released movie *A Perfect World* (starring Clint Eastwood as a Ranger), the television series *Walker, Texas Ranger*, and the innumerable movies and books preceding them. As such, the movement to overhaul the Texas Rangers, and the Rangers' cynical and defensive reaction to that movement, are knotted together in our state's tangled web of romance and realpolitik, honor and progress, myth and mortality. The knot is what binds us, and what forms the noose we cannot slip.

A RETIRED RANGER STARED DREAMILY AT THE plaque he kept on his wall, bearing the name of his most famous predecessors. "Leander McNelly," he murmured at last, and his voice almost caved in with emotion as he quoted one of McNelly's men, "Lord, how I would have charged hell with a handbucket behind the leadership of that man!"

Rangers are faithful keepers of Ranger mythology, and it all begins with McNelly, the youthful captain under whose command a pintsize brigade slaughtered countless criminals and Mexicans from 1874 until 1877. To the Rangers and their admiring historians, McNelly is an appealing composite of warlord and Christ figure: courageous and gentlemanly, utterly

DISTINCTIVE MERIT AWARDS

ANOTHER DAY AT THE BORDER

*In Rwanda this summer,
caricatures of life
in the mass production
of death.*

PHOTOGRAPH BY JAMES NACHTWEY
TEXT BY JIM WOOTEN

ALL DAY LONG IN THE SIMMERING sun, a river of Rwandan refugees flows relentlessly north from Goma, a decrepit little town in eastern Zaire, toward a hulking range of volcanoes. One bare foot after the other, they plod wearily on, as though they all have appointments at the end of the world, somewhere far beyond the thousands of bodies that line the road for the next 25 miles — bodies abandoned without burial in this desolate corner of Africa as inhospitable to the dead as to the living, a thin sifting of black talcum over a bed of black rock.

As the road rises, the temperature falls and most of the corpses lack the straw mats or blankets customarily used to wrap them. On this chilly moonscape, the living have more need of them, though without their shrouds the dead have stiffened into sad caricatures of life: a mother and child reaching for each other, a man sitting against a tree, a woman with arms stretched upward as though welcoming a lover.

In Kibumba, the largest and most wretched of the three refugee camps, the bodies are piled into huge, precarious pyramids that are then dismantled by snarling front loaders lifting and dumping them into vast trenches dug by bulldozers. Near Goma, a dump truck moves slowly along as teams of Rwandan men heave the bodies into the back. It is an ugly metaphor, but they seem to be collecting Africa's trash.

At a banana grove, the truck backs up to a trench. Half the length of a football field, half full of dead refugees. A horrific sprawl of arms intertwined with legs interwoven with torsos bent at mad angles. A baby seems comfortably asleep in the crook of an elderly man's arm. A pregnant woman's hands are locked around her swollen abdomen. The air is thick with the sickeningly sweet smell of death.

With a hydraulic whine, the truck bed rises and tilts, and for a long frozen moment nothing happens. Somehow, the bodies defy the physics of the nearly perpendicular angle. Then, in a rush, a hundred former human beings descend together into the crowded trench, beyond tribal vendettas, beyond politics, beyond murder, beyond madness forever.

There is no dignity here.
There is too much death here for dignity. ∎

60

Distinctive Merit/National

FULL PAGE OR SPREAD
Another Day at the Border
ART DIRECTOR *Janet Froelich*
DESIGNER *Nancy Harris*
PHOTO EDITOR *Kathy Ryan*
PHOTOGRAPHER *James Nachtwey*
CLIENT *The New York Times Magazine*

(facing page, top)
Distinctive Merit/National

FULL PAGE OR SPREAD
A Domestic Moment
ART DIRECTOR *Tom Bentkowski*
DESIGNER *Jean Andreuzzi*
DIRECTOR OF PHOTOGRAPHY *David Friend*
PHOTOGRAPHER *Joseph Rodriguez*
CLIENT *Life Magazine*

(facing page, bottom)
Distinctive Merit/National

FULL PAGE OR SPREAD
Worse than Death
ART DIRECTOR *Tom Bentkowski*
DESIGNER *Jean Andreuzzi*
DIRECTOR OF PHOTOGRAPHY *David Friend*
PHOTO EDITOR *Barbara Baker Burrows*
PHOTOGRAPHER *Glenn Hartung*
CLIENT *Life Magazine*

The **BIG** Picture

A tender domestic moment: One-year-old Jacqueline sits on a gun-littered carpet while Daddy shows her how to hold a pistol and Mommy smiles with fond approval. Such is life in East Los Angeles, a violent barrio where sidearms are as common as boom boxes and inspire almost as casual a reaction. In any reasonable world a mother would gasp, *Get that gun out of my baby's hand!* But Yvonne, whose man belongs to a powerful street gang, does not live in a reasonable world. And let's face it, neither do the rest of us.

America today is an armed camp, with 67 million handguns in circulation. Every year some 640,000 of us are confronted by a criminal with a handgun, and violence begets violence as fear of guns sells more guns in an endless feedback loop. All too often the casualties are children. Each day 13 youngsters are killed by guns and 30 others are wounded; in 1991 alone, 5,356 died. We are murdering the future, and the trigger is often pulled by a child. Our schools, where tens of thousands of guns are carried to class every day, have become a killing ground.

We have a choice: Give up guns or give up lives. And after years of dithering, we're showing symptoms of resolve: the Brady bill, Jesse Jackson's Save the Children campaign, a few programs that offer cash and amnesty for unlicensed firearms—and there's that ingenious toys-for-guns exchange that recently harvested almost 1,000 firearms in a single New York City police precinct. The idea has caught on in other cities, and that's good news. It won't rip out the social, economic and emotional roots of violence, but it will save some lives, and it may give children like Jacqueline a bunny instead of a trigger to squeeze.

—CLAUDIA GLENN DOWLING

12

JOSEPH RODRIGUEZ/BLACK STAR

The **BIG** Picture

Worse than Death

It began on a quiet Sunday morning when sparks from a faulty wire turned a Cincinnati home into an inferno. Dennis Rogers, 22, rushed out of the house but then plunged back into the flames to save his children, Shawn, three, and Sadie, six months. Overcome by smoke and critically burned, he was pulled from the pyre more dead than alive. When Rogers finally regained consciousness, he learned the full extent of the disaster. Firefighters had managed to save Shawn, but Sadie had not survived.

OPEN HERE

GLENN HARTONG/THE CINCINNATI ENQUIRER

Distinctive Merit/National

FULL PAGE OR SPREAD
What's New York the Capital of Now?
ART DIRECTOR *Janet Froelich*
DESIGNER *Cathy Gilmore-Barnes*
PHOTO EDITOR *Kathy Ryan*
PHOTOGRAPHER *Michael O'Neill*
CLIENT *The New York Times Magazine*

ADDITIONAL AWARD

Merit
**GRAPHIC DESIGN, EDITORIAL DESIGN,
MAGAZINE, CONSUMER OR BUSINESS, FULL ISSUE**

Distinctive Merit/National

FULL PAGE OR SPREAD
DJ Red Alert
CREATIVE DIRECTOR *Fred Woodward*
PHOTO EDITOR *Denise Sfraga*
PHOTOGRAPHER *Alicia Exum*
CLIENT *Rolling Stone*

(facing page, top)
Distinctive Merit/National

FULL PAGE OR SPREAD
Skate Till You Die
CREATIVE DIRECTOR *Fred Woodward*
DESIGNER *Lee Bearson*
PHOTO EDITOR *Denise Sfraga*
PHOTO ILLUSTRATION *Alicia Exum*
CLIENT *Rolling Stone*

(facing page, bottom)
Distinctive Merit/National

FULL PAGE OR SPREAD
Carrot Top
CREATIVE DIRECTOR *Fred Woodward*
DESIGNER *Fred Woodward*
PHOTO EDITOR *Jodi Peckman*
PHOTOGRAPHER *Mark Seliger*
CLIENT *Rolling Stone*

PHOTO ILLUSTRATION BY EKUM

<BY PETER WILKINSON>

SKATE TILL YOU DIE

>> THE FAST TIMES AND TRAGIC >> DEATH OF JEFF PHILLIPS, THE KING OF TEXAS SKATEBOARDING >>

HE FRIENDS OF JEFF PHIL-
lips gathered around a
VCR to pay tribute. It was
the night of Dec. 29, 1993,
in Dallas. Someone put a
video from 1988 in the machine. Most
of the mourners, Johnson included,
were professional skateboarders, and
since they'd been drinking beer and
Cuervo for hours, they hooted when
they saw their images on the TV. From
the mantel, a blown-up color photograph of Jeff looked down: Jeff with the
unruly mop of brown hair, the high
cheekbones and meager stubble, the
wide-set, weary eyes.

The room fell silent. There he was on
the screen: tall, square-shouldered,
graceful Jeff at 6 feet 2 inches, looking
huge on the ramp, muscling himself
back and forth in the half-pipe, gather-
ing speed. He rode backward up to the
lip, planted his hand, swung himself
completely upside down, then shifted
his weight, twisted around and dropped
back onto the ramp. A perfect Phillips
66: his signature maneuver, the one few
other skaters could ever do.

In the dim light of Craig Johnson's
living room, Jeff skated again. Then,
with the push of a button, he was gone.

As they grieved in the days following
his death, Jeff's friends talked about how
adulthood always mystified him and
seemed blissfully out of his reach. Jeff
thought maturity confined you like a
necktie. "Why grow up?" he would ask.
"Just because somebody says?"

Even at 30, Jeff, winner of three
national skateboarding competitions,
still lived a boy's life. He skated all the
time, wildly, powerfully, balls out, as
they say in Texas. In his little house
atop a wooded hill in northeast Dallas,
Jeff pulled frequent all-nighters, building models of spaceships and Japanese
cartoon heroes, painting and gluing
alongside glass tanks filled with snakes,
chameleons, spiders, lizards and turtles.
If Jeff needed to think, he climbed 60
feet up a nearby sycamore to a plywood
treehouse – his favorite sanctuary.

Jeff spent a lot of time in the treehouse in 1993. The indoor skateboard
park he owned was losing money. Alison
Young, the ethereal blonde who had
been his girlfriend for 10 years, had
moved out of their house to a place of
her own. He was depressed for good
reasons. But none of his friends could
have predicted that Jeff would take a
.357 Magnum and shoot himself in the
head early Christmas Day.

A few days after the funeral, Alison
was packing up Jeff's belongings. She
dragged his mattress out to the street for
a Salvation Army pickup. Skaters from
all over the country and Mexico kept
calling, asking the same difficult question: "What was up with the dude?"
Alison searched for an answer. "It's like

ROLLING STONE, SEPTEMBER 8, 1994 · 57

Carrot Top's
jokes deal
with college
concerns
like getting
drunk
and laid.

"Eventually
I'm going
to outgrow
this," he says.
"But I connect
with them
pretty well."

It's Show Time!

By RICH COHEN

"'RIP THIS JOINT' – LET'S HEAR IT!" yells Mick Jagger, looking like a sinister emergency-room surgeon with his loose-fitting green pants and end-of-the-day facial expression. His weary voice fills the school gym on the edge of Toronto where the Rolling Stones have gathered to rehearse for their 1994-'95 world tour, and for a long moment after Jagger has made his request, the other Stones stand in a sort of furrowed silence, like men trying to hear

The ROLLING STONES are taking their rock & roll circus back on the road.

But is it still the greatest show on earth?

PHOTOGRAPHS BY ANTON CORBIJN

"I got news for you," says Richards. "We're still a bunch of tough bastards. String us up and we still won't die."

These days, when Jagger sings about satisfaction, he may be thinking less of willing teen-age girls than of the neat aesthetics of a well-turned deal.

Battered by misfortune, the walls of tradition that defend the Old Colony faith have crumbled at critical points. In Mexico as in Canada, some young Mennonites have discovered the secular pleasures of beer drinking, pop music and pre-marital sex. The stress that comes with change has even provoked occasional domestic violence among these peaceful people. And some have forsaken the faith because they cannot bear its burdens. But in many families, especially those in the Mexican colonies, children like eight-year-old Helen Dyck (right), a cousin of the four T-shirted sisters on page 91, grow up in homes suffused with spiritual radiance. At the center of these families stands a powerful religious belief, and that center continues to hold. □

96

(facing page)
Distinctive Merit/National

SERIES
The Rolling Stones
CREATIVE DIRECTOR *Fred Woodward*
DESIGNERS *Fred Woodward, Lee Bearson*
PHOTO EDITOR *Jodi Peckman*
PHOTOGRAPHER *Anton Corbijn*
CLIENT *Rolling Stone*

(right)
Distinctive Merit/National

SERIES
Mennonites: Endless Exodus
ART DIRECTOR *Tom Bentkowski*
DESIGNER *Tom Bentkowski*
DIRECTOR OF PHOTOGRAPHY *David Friend*
PHOTOGRAPHER *Larry Towell*
CLIENT *Life Magazine*

94   95

JOURNEY

The world of the Old Colony Mennonites is a well-preserved slice of 16th century life. Rejecting progress as ungodly, living in a closed society, the faithful dress, work, speak and worship like Germans of the Reformation era. To preserve their way of life, they fled from Europe to Canada in the last century, then moved on to Mexico in the 1920s. There they farmed in biblical simplicity until drought and cheap U.S. produce killed their livelihood. Looking for jobs, hundreds of destitute families have now returned to Canada, where many toil in the fields for third-world wages. **Larry Towell** has documented on film this latest stage in their

E N D L E S S
EXODUS

90   Reporting by JOSH SIMON

489

Distinctive Merit/National

SERIES
Scotland by the Yard
ART DIRECTOR *Janet Froelich*
DESIGNER *Lisa Naftolin*
PHOTOGRAPHER *Sarah Moon*
CLIENT *The New York Times Magazine*

(facing page)
Distinctive Merit/National

GRAPHIC DESIGN, SERIES
Erickson's Self-Promotion Mailer
ART DIRECTOR *Jeff Griffith*
DESIGNER *Jeff Griffith*
COPYWRITER *Larry Bennett*
PHOTOGRAPHER *Jim Erickson*
PRODUCER *Suzanne Moore*
AGENCY *Griffith Advertising Design*
CLIENT *Erickson Production*

Merit/International

SERIES
Skin, Boys, Swimmer
ART DIRECTOR *Warren Eakins*
COPYWRITER *Evelyn Monroe*
PHOTOGRAPHER *Nadav Kander*
AGENCY *Wieden & Kennedy, Amsterdam*
CLIENT *Nike*

Merit/National

FULL PAGE OR SPREAD
Brassica
ART DIRECTOR *Gael Towey*
DESIGNER *Claudia Bruno*
PHOTOGRAPHER *Maria Robledo*
CLIENT *Martha Stewart Living*

Merit/National

FULL PAGE OR SPREAD
Chickens
ART DIRECTOR *Gael Towey*
DESIGNER *Gael Towey*
PHOTOGRAPHER *Victor Schrager*
CLIENT *Martha Stewart Living*

Merit/National

FULL PAGE OR SPREAD
The Cranberries
CREATIVE DIRECTOR *Fred Woodward*
PHOTO EDITORS *Jodi Peckman, Fiona McDonagh*
PHOTOGRAPHER *Raymond Meeks*
CLIENT *Rolling Stone*

Merit/National

FULL PAGE OR SPREAD
Perry Farrell
CREATIVE DIRECTOR *Fred Woodward*
PHOTO EDITOR *Jodi Peckman*
PHOTOGRAPHER *Mark Seliger*
CLIENT *Rolling Stone*

(facing page, top)
Merit/National

FULL PAGE OR SPREAD
Seinfeld
CREATIVE DIRECTOR *Fred Woodward*
DESIGNERS *Fred Woodward, Gail Anderson*
PHOTO EDITOR *Jodi Peckman*
PHOTOGRAPHER *Mark Seliger*
CLIENT *Rolling Stone*

(facing page, bottom)
Merit/National

FULL PAGE OR SPREAD
Anaconda
ART DIRECTOR *Tom Bentkowski*
DESIGNER *Mimi Park*
DIRECTOR OF PHOTOGRAPHY *David Friend*
PHOTOGRAPHER *James Balog*
CLIENT *Life Magazine*

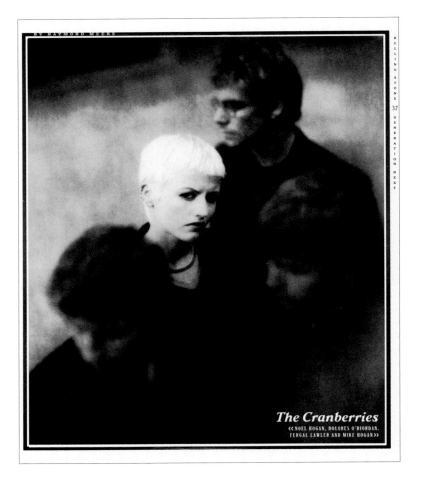

The KING of Prime-Time COMEDY by Fred Schruers

Photographs by MARK SELIGER

Rolling Stone, September 22, 1994 · 47

IMAGINE A 30-FOOT,
300-POUND CORSET
THAT TIGHTENS EACH
TIME YOU EXHALE.
THAT'S HOW AN
ANACONDA SLOWLY
SUFFOCATES A
VICTIM, BE IT A SIX-
FOOT ALLIGATOR OR A
SIX-FOOT SWIMMER.
AT LEAST AN
ANACONDA WAITS
UNTIL IT NO LONGER
FEELS LIFE BEFORE
SWALLOWING ITS
MEAL—WHOLE.
ALTHOUGH IT CANNOT
SWALLOW ANYTHING
AS BULKY AS AN
ADULT HUMAN, THAT
IS NO CONSOLATION
TO THE PERSON
THE ANACONDA HAS
SUFFOCATED.

SERIES
Woodstock
ART DIRECTOR *Tom Bentkowski*
DESIGNER *Marti Golon*
DIRECTOR OF PHOTOGRAPHY *David Friend*
PHOTOGRAPHER *Gregory Heisler*
CLIENT *Life Magazine*

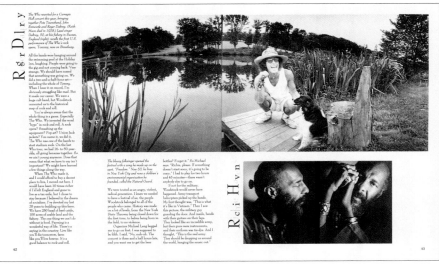

Merit/National

SERIES
Cindy Crawford
CREATIVE DIRECTOR *Fred Woodward*
DESIGNER *Fred Woodward*
PHOTO EDITOR *Laurie Kratochvil*
PHOTOGRAPHER *Herb Ritts*
CLIENT *Rolling Stone*

Merit/National

SERIES
Gang Wars
ART DIRECTOR *D. J. Stout*
DESIGNERS *D. J. Stout, Nancy McMillan*
COPYWRITER *Audrey Duff*
PHOTOGRAPHER *Dan Winters*
CLIENT *Texas Monthly*

"WE GET ALL HYPED UP, WE DO A DRIVE-BY" A REPORT FROM THE FRONT LINES OF THE SAN ANTONIO GANG WARS.

PHOTOGRAPHS BY DAN WINTERS

BY AUDREY DUFF

T'S ONE-FIFTEEN IN THE MORNING ON A Sunday in May. At the Alazan Apache Courts, one of San Antonio's toughest housing projects, seven teenage boys wearing designer jeans and polo shirts huddle behind the fence and garbage dumpster that separate the rear courtyard from the street. The boys crack jokes and suck down forty-ounce bottles of malt liquor.

The cover is decent here. They can see the street through the fence, and they have memorized every car in the neighborhood and its owner. Anyone cruising by looking to shoot somebody would have difficulty aiming into the shadows of the Courts. The boys, ranging in age from sixteen to eighteen, are members of three different gangs that get along—usually. They

LAST YEAR, THERE WERE 3.5 DRIVE-BY SHOOTINGS A DAY IN SAN ANTONIO, SAYS A POLICEMAN: "PEOPLE ARE AFRAID TO GO OUTSIDE."

lean against the dumpster or sit with their backs against a concrete wall. Just blocks away live their "enemies," members of rival gangs from neighboring housing projects: the Cassiano Homes, the San Juan Homes, the Villa Veramendi, and the Victoria Courts, all warring fiefdoms clustered on San Antonio's West Side.

"You always got to watch your back," says one of the boys, a sixteen-year-old who joined his first gang when he was eleven. He chats amiably about what he and his friends do for fun. "We get really drunk," he says. "We get all hyped up, and we do a drive-by or something like that."

TEXAS MONTHLY 133

At that moment, five shots rip through the air, and he and the others fall silent. The shots were loud and close. All seven boys start running through the rear courtyard—toward the gunfire. If the shooters make another pass, the boys can see who it is.

The boys backtrack through the soggy yard, where laundry hangs from clotheslines and the grass needs cutting, and they are a little edgier than they were before. Behind a sagging sheet, a dark figure approaches the boys with a gleaming gun in his hand. He yells something in Spanish as he points the gun at them and slides back the chamber. Is this it?

The moment is tense, but the boy turns out to be a friend. The others laugh at his performance and return to their spots against the wall and the dumpster, but something has changed. The air is electric. They chuckle and say they are not afraid. "Things like that happen here all the time," says one. Mean-

while, the teenager with the gun paces around the periphery of the group, watching their backs.

No one got hurt that night, but the incident brings into relief the two San Antonios: one a thriving city of beauty, history, and culture that draws tourists from around the country, and the other a city of warring youths, where small children are killed in their beds by stray gunfire. In 1993 there were 1,262 drive-by shootings reported in San Antonio, which has a population of 935,933. (The police department estimates that for every drive-by that is reported, ten are not.) In contrast, Dallas, with a population of 1,007,618, reported 221 drive-by shootings last year. Fort Worth's police department recorded 186 drive-bys, and in Austin there were an estimated 50. (Houston and El Paso don't keep figures on drive-by shootings but group them with homicides or assaults.)

"People are afraid to go outside. Children are afraid to play outside," says San Antonio police officer George Saxton. Until recently, Saxton patrolled Military Drive, a favorite Sunday-night cruising strip on the South Side where gang members go to meet girls. Gun-toting teens routinely turn the strip into a war zone. Says Saxton: "Drive-bys are the biggest fear we have in this town."

MARKY SITS AT THE KITCHEN table of his family's three-bedroom apartment at the Alazan Apache Courts, where he lives with his mother, elder brother, younger sister, and sister-in-law. His brown eyes are still droopy at eleven-fifteen on a weekday morning because, he says, he heard shots outside his home late last night and got up to investigate. Marky lives on the West Side, where the Hispanic gangs predominate.

Marky's sister-in-law, who is 21 years old and seven months' pregnant, sits on the couch in the living room watching soap operas on TV. A mirror and a print of flowers on the wall behind her hide only a few of the dozen or so bullet holes in the wall.

"The first time we got shot up, it was my mom and her boyfriend sitting in here," Marky says, yawning and rubbing his beefy neck. "The guys who did it were looking for me and my older brother because we were LA Boys and these guys were Kings. They were 'forks down' and we were 'forks up.'"

The sign of a pitchfork—made with the thumb, index finger, and middle finger—pointing either up or down indicates which of the two broad alliances of San Antonio's Hispanic gangs a particular gang belongs to. Gangs that use forks down are in the Black Circle; those that use forks up are in the Blue Circle. Wearing "colors," such as black or blue bandannas (called rags), can also tip off gang members as to who their friends are. And each individual gang has its own set of hand signs, usually the first letter of the gang's name.

Marky joined the LA Boys, named by Lanier High School football players who used the Lanier Athletics logo for their name, when he was in the seventh grade. "Me and my best friend wanted to get in because they had a lot of parties and a

GUNS AND POSES: AFTER GANG MEMBERS PICK OUT THEIR WEAPONS IN PAWNSHOPS OR GUN SHOWS, A FRIEND WHO IS OVER 21 BUYS THEM. GANG MEMBERS AREN'T ALWAYS YOUTHFUL—THE MAN ABOVE IS IN HIS THIRTIES—BUT THE YOUNGEST CAN BE THE MOST DANGEROUS, ACCORDING TO THE POLICE. "I REMEMBER THE FIRST TIME I SHOT A REAL GUN," SAYS MARKY, SIXTEEN (TOP LEFT—WITH AN ASSAULT RIFLE—AND RIGHT). "IT'S LIKE A HIGH . . ." EVERY GANG HAS ITS SYMBOLS: MARKY'S TATTOOS, TWEETY AND "O INC." PROCLAIM PAST AFFILIATIONS; AT LEFT, A MEMBER OF THE NO POSSE WEARING A NOTRE DAME CAP SHOWS OFF A STAB WOUND.

TEXAS MONTHLY 135

OPPOSITE: A TEENAGER SHOWS OFF HIS PIECE TO A FORMER GANG MEMBER (LEFT). THE HISPANIC GANGS ARE DIVIDED INTO TWO BROAD ALLIANCES; THE SIGN OF A PITCHFORK POINTING EITHER UP OR DOWN INDICATES WHICH ONE A GANG BELONGS TO. "FORKS DOWN"—SHOWN AS A GRAFFITI (ABOVE LEFT) AND A HAND SIGN "THROWN" BY A GANG MEMBER (ABOVE)—MEANS ALLEGIANCE TO THE BLACK CIRCLE. THROWING HAND SIGNS AT A RIVAL GANG CAN TRIGGER A DRIVE-BY SHOOTING. GANG MEMBERS ALSO ANNOUNCE THEIR LOYALTIES BY WEARING THEIR GANG'S "COLORS"—A BANDANNA, OR "RAG," LEFT: A MEMBER OF THE NO POSSE SHOWS HIS COLORS.

lot of chicks," he says. "We had to get rolled in [beaten up] by about fifteen guys in the plaza right here at the Courts for initiation, but my dad had always kicked my ass, so I didn't give a shit. This one huge guy looked at my friend Juan, so I thought he was going to hit him, but he went *pow* and I hit the wall and bounced off it, and he kept hitting me, and I didn't know how, but I got up, and they all beat me into a corner. Afterward they said, 'You made it. You can cry now.' But I didn't want to cry."

When Marky was thirteen, he quit the LA Boys and joined Damage, Inc. He strips off his shirt to display his tattoos—proof of his allegiance. On his left shoulder is a yellow Tweety bird clutching a handgun, left over from the days when he belonged to the LA Boys. Beneath the heavily armed bird is another tattoo: D Inc.

By the time Marky was fourteen, he had taken part in several drive-by shootings. Drive-bys are almost always committed by organized street gangs. Anything can trigger a drive-by—a turf battle, a squabble over a girlfriend, "throwing" hand signs at rival gangs, an initiation, or the sheer thrill of it. "Drive-bys start when people from another gang act big shit and be, like, 'You're nobody,'" Marky explains, "and some people get serious and get out the guns."

Gang members get their guns from pawnshops or gun shows; after they pick out their weapons, a companion who is over 21 buys them. "I remember the first time I shot a real gun," Marky murmurs with a faraway look in his eyes. "It's like a high, and you like it, and you want to do it again and again and again. I don't remember doing my first drive-by—that was a long time ago. But I remember using my first Tec-9

[a semi-automatic pistol]. We were driving around and we said, 'Let's hit up some houses.' I was on the passenger side and they said, 'Go, Mark! Go!' I just shot like that—*pow-pow-pow!*" Marky points his right hand out to the side and jerks it high in the air. "It was kicking, and I didn't know it would do that. My friends thought that was cool, but they were all scared too."

Marky says he regrets one drive-by that killed innocent people. "We went to the wrong house. It was like the house was all shady and shit. I saw it on the news. They didn't like. I felt bad about it. I didn't want to think about it." He looks away and frowns. "I don't think about it."

Explaining why he participates in "gangbanging"—a word that in his milieu describes not gang rape but a long list of activities that includes beating people up, stealing cars, throw-

ing hand signs to incite rival gangs, and doing drive-bys—Marky says, "It's fun. It's exciting. We get crazy. Everybody thinks I come from a messed-up family and my mom don't love me and shit like that, but that's not it."

Still, Marky describes a childhood filled with physical abuse. "My dad used to hit me, and my mother would just watch or go to her room and shut the door. I stole money from my grandmother when I was little to buy soda and candy—twenty bucks. She told my dad, and he beat the shit out of me. He always wore boots, so he used to kick me when I was down. I once told him, 'Hit me when you're sober, why don't you?'" Marky has not seen his father in four years.

OFFICER RICK ROJAS IS A LARGE MAN who is quick to laugh at any joke, but after three years in the trenches of gang warfare in San Antonio, his good humor is wearing thin. "They're all a bunch of dumb kids," Rojas says with a sigh. "They may do some horrible crimes, but it's easy to catch them because they think like kids."

The 35-year-old Rojas is a member of the San Antonio Police Department's gang unit, which was formed in June 1991. The gang unit saturates trouble spots with patrolling officers and mobile police cruisers. Its sixteen members pho-

TEXAS MONTHLY 137

The Black Garden

Photographs by Jason Eskenazi

A moment of prayer for those killed in an attempted coup two days before in Freedom Square, Grozny, capital of the Chechen Republic

Elderly Abkhazians wait in line to convert their money from the useless Georgian currency into Russian rubles

A gardener working by a statue of Stalin and a headless Lenin in the front yard of a hospital in Sukhumi

For tens of thousands of years men have fought battles over territory. They fought across rivers and for towns they thought they were once mandated to have. For whatever the outcome both the victims and victors have long ago dissolved back into the soil of their ancestors. Where ancient battles were fought, new ones arise over the same landscape.

Few memories last more than two generations. It is no great advantage that our civilization has the photographic medium to remember and record and preserve this collective and personal memory through the lens. Because with the world so small today all battles fought affect us all. It is said that the camera eye is interested in all that is pointed at but it is the photographer that must choose the subject.

Take a Caucasus journey to a region between the Black and Caspian Seas, where since the breakup of the former Soviet Union, tensions in Georgia, Armenia, Azerbaijan, and southern Russia have escalated into numerous conflicts. The battles are fought against a backdrop of old world traditions. The regions are experiencing the

same horrors of Yugoslavia, but without the world's focus on them. Nearly all who walk the streets of these conflict zones comment on the beauty of the ravaged landscape where no family goes untouched. The victors are indistinguishable from the victims.

In December of 1991, the Georgian capital, Tbilisi, was being destroyed by battles between forces loyal to the first democratically elected president, Zviad Gamsakhurdia, and those who charged that he was a dictator. The downtown was destroyed. The President fled. Meanwhile in Abkhazia, a western Georgian territory situated on the Black Sea, Abkhazian separatists were gearing up to retake the land though they only comprised 18% of the population. Abkhazians, backed by the Russian army, steered a course to nationhood through a peace brokerage by the Russians. Now, as the Abkhazians reinhabit the place that means "land of lost souls" they try to repair Sukhumi, the Georgian capital they have occupied. It is a tenuous peace always waiting for the threatened return by Edvard Shevardnadze, the Georgian president.

In Baku's backyard stands Azerbaijan's oldest oil field where rotting wood and rusty sheets of metal protect many people living in the freedom oil field located on the Illeych Bay of the Caspian Sea. Large and small stones weigh down the roofs of houses from the strong sea wind where residents seem oblivious to this wasteland of black water, oil smells, and the constant creak, thump, and squeal of aged oil wells. For these people their newly found independence has meant war in the disputed enclave of Nagorno-Karabakh.

Karabakh's capital, Stepanakert, is the site of daily bombings and funeral processions. Its residents keep an ear to the ground and an eye on the sky because there is no warning system as people react to bombing hits from Azeri planes. This city, which previously produced fifteen daily births, now sees only two newborns daily and buries at least two victims of the fighting daily.

In northwest Azerbaijan we come upon Krasnayasloboda, the "Red Village." The old men who gather on the main street can hear the echoes of the Muslim Koran being read as they drink their tea and play

endless games of backgammon. We are a resurgence of practicing Judaism that had been quelled during the Soviet era. These mountain Jews have their roots in Iran and speak a dialect of Farsi called Tati. For over 1,000 years they have inhabited mountain villages in the Caucasus and only in the last 250 years have they resettled in the cities leaving behind only three aged cemeteries. In 1938 it is said that 17 rabbis were massacred in a Stalin pogrom that drove Judaism underground for over 40 years. Where once there were 11 synagogues, the service continues in the last surviving one.

The Caucasus is the forgotten gem of civilization that was Jason's Land of the Golden Fleece. It is still a prisoner of its Soviet past. Now that the Russians seek greater control over its Caucasus neighbor, it seems less likely that a peaceful fruit can ever be cultivated in this black garden.

JASON ESKENAZI

Merit/National

SERIES
The Black Garden
ART DIRECTOR *Jill Korostoff*
DIRECTOR OF PHOTOGRAPHY *Peter Howe*
PHOTOGRAPHER *Jason Eskenazi*
CLIENT *Outtakes*

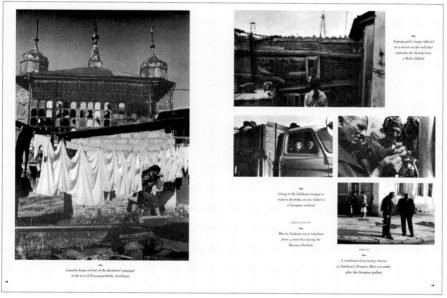

A young girl's image reflected in a mirror on the wall that separates her family from a Baku Oilfield

Going to the Sukhumi morgue to reclaim the bodies of sons killed in a Georgian ambush

ABOVE RIGHT
Men in Gulauta try to telephone from a street box during the Russian blockade

ABOVE
A semblance of normalcy returns to Sukhumi's Prospect Mira two weeks after the Georgian pullout

Laundry hangs in front of the abandoned synagogue in the town of Krasnayasloboda, Azerbaijan

LEFT
A young mother and three children flee the bombing in Stepanakert on a helicopter to Yerevan

BELOW
The bodies of 126 soldiers were Recovered in a mass grave behind the hospital in Sukhumi six months after a Georgian ambush

BELOW
The Freedom Oil Field, where Stalin organized his first strikes

A woman mourns the death of her brother in Tbilisi

An orphan lies isolated in Kharkent near Yerevan

A soldier searches for the body of his brother in Sukhumi

A mourning ceremony in Krasnayasloboda

Merit/National

SERIES
From Russia, with Hope and Fear
ART DIRECTOR *Janet Froelich*
DESIGNER *Nancy Harris*
PHOTO EDITOR *Kathy Ryan*
PHOTOGRAPHER *Sebastião Salgado*
CLIENT *The New York Times Magazine*

FROM RUSSIA, WITH HOPE AND FEAR

BRIGHTON BEACH IS NO PARADISE FOR NEWLY ARRIVED RUSSIANS. BUT IT'S A START. AND FOR IMMIGRANTS, THAT'S WHAT NEW YORK HAS ALWAYS BEEN ABOUT.

IT'S STRANGELY LIKE RUSSIA: THE CHATTER, THE LINES AT THE MARKETS, THE AWKWARD HIPNESS OF THE TEEN-AGERS, THE DRAB DRESS OF THE ELDERS.

THE HAUNTING CITY
LIFE AND DEATH IN BENARAS

Photographs by Mary Ellen Mark

India has been dominant in my work since my first trip there in the late sixties. It has been the source for three of my books, *Falkland Road* (1980), *Mother Theresa's Missions of Charity* (1985), and *Indian Circus* (1993). Last year I produced a documentary film photographed and directed by my husband, Martin Bell, *The Amazing Plastic Lady*, about a traveling circus in South India.

India is the country that fascinates me most—the country that draws me back to complete projects started many years ago. Benaras is one of them. For me it is the most haunting city in India, full of mystery and passion. It is a city of life. It is a city of death.

The demands of my professional life in New York are difficult and stressful. At such times I imagine myself in Benaras, pretending I am on a boat floating down the Ganges. It is late afternoon. As my boat travels past the ghats, the stairways leading to the river, I imagine songs, chants, ringing bells, prayers and lowing cows. Twilight fades into the darkness and slowly lights appear from the ancient buildings along the river's edge. The glimmering candles bobbing on the water give the early evening atmosphere a ghostly and eerie quality. I'm suffused by the smell of jasmine garlands. All is peace. There is no place I would rather be.

The photographs in this portfolio were taken over a quarter of a century. Benaras is visually rich and yields images of wide-ranging subject matter. There are photographs of hippies of the 'sixties' who visited the city in their search for spiritualism and drugs. I photographed real sadhus and fake sadhus, body builders, blind children and even a maharajah. I see these not merely as reflections of an exotic country, but photographs that cross cultural boundaries and reflect the universality of human experience. As in all my work, I aim for design, atmosphere, and spontaneity, but most important to me is developing personal photographic intimacy with my subjects.

Benaras is most famous for the daily bathing and cremation rituals along the river ghats. I not only photographed that lively activity, but the more private workings of the people and the city. I made pictures at the Mani Karam Burning Ghat which is an essential aspect of life in Benaras. I also tried to show these people performing the rituals that accompany the death ceremony. In some cases, I photographed people just before death in their hospice-like dwellings in the city.

This is an incomplete body of work. I dream of returning to Benaras for an extended time to finish it and eventually produce a book. Five years ago, on my final day of photographing in Benaras, I said goodbye to one of the woodcutters at the Mani Karam Burning Ghat. "Nice to meet you," he said. "Be sure and come back here when you die."

MARY ELLEN MARK

Merit/National

SERIES
The Haunting City
ART DIRECTOR *Jill Korostoff*
DIRECTOR OF PHOTOGRAPHY *Peter Howe*
PHOTOGRAPHER *Mary Ellen Mark*
CLIENT *Outtakes*

ADDITIONAL AWARD

Merit
FULL PAGE OR SPREAD

"I see these not merely as reflections of an exotic country, but photographs which cross cultural boundaries and reflect the universality of human experience."

"I said goodbye to one of the woodcutters at the Mani Karam Burning Ghat. 'Nice to meet you' he said, 'Be sure and come back here when you die'."

(left)
Merit/National

SERIES
The Capital Call Girls
ART DIRECTOR *D. J. Stout*
DESIGNERS *D. J. Stout, Nancy McMillan*
COPYWRITER *Robert Draper*
PHOTOGRAPHER *Dan Winters*
CLIENT *Texas Monthly*

(facing page, top)
Merit/National

SERIES
Redwoods Forever
ART DIRECTOR *Lou DiLorenzo*
DESIGNER *Diane Bertolo*
PHOTO EDITOR *Bill Black*
PHOTOGRAPHER *Karen Kuehn*
CLIENT *Travel Holiday*

(facing page, bottom)
Merit/International

SERIES
Der Weg nach oben
ART DIRECTOR *Sigi Mayer*
COPYWRITER *Sigi Mayer*
PHOTOGRAPHER *Horst Stasny*
STUDIO *Sigi Mayer*
CLIENT *Modern Times*

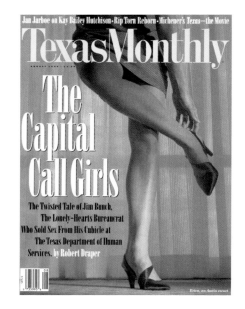

Logged or loved, the earth's
oldest, noblest trees may outlive
all our quarrels over them

Redwoods Forever

In most travel guides, "northern California" means the San Francisco Bay area, the cultural counterweight to Los Angeles. But these longtime rivals have far more in common with each other than either has with the real northern California—a vast backcountry where you can drive for 200 miles in the nation's most populous state without

encountering a town with as many as 30,000 people. Cross the Golden Gate, leave the suburbs and the wineries behind, and you will enter a California that has never quite shared in the golden dream that is the state's formative myth. It is gorgeous terrain, rugged and rural, but its climax forests and swift rivers have always been regarded more benignly by visitors than by home folks, to whom the forests represent the main source of livelihood and the rivers represent a threat of killer floods. So remote is this

In Lady Bird Johnson Grove, at Redwood National Park (left), the life cycles of an infant child and a centuries-old tree converge. A wall in Fern Canyon (above).

by **PAUL BURKA** · *photographed by* **KAREN KUEHN**

APRIL 1994 **81**

der weg nach oben

*eine lyrische modestory,
erzählt von sigi mayer (concept) & horst stasny (foto)*

1789m seehöhe

fashion by setball

509

Merit/National

FULL PAGE OR SPREAD
Dinner Invitation Announcement Poster
ART DIRECTOR *Bob Gill*
PHOTOGRAPHER *Carl Fischer*
CLIENT *The Art Directors Club*

OPEN *to* SUGGESTION

WHETHER THEY WORK IN METAL, NYLON OR LACE, DESIGNERS LOVE PLAYING PEEKABOO.

NYLON MESH T-SHIRT, $35 *At Chartreuse, 18 West 57th Street. Wire mannequars by Samuel Rothvury.*
TEXTURED STOCKINGS *by DKNY, $15. At Macy's. Pumps by Michel Perry.*

THE NEW YORK TIMES MAGAZINE / NOVEMBER 13, 1994 71

Silver Medalist/National

SERIES
Open to Suggestion
ART DIRECTOR *Janet Froelich*
DESIGNER *Lisa Naftolin*
ILLUSTRATOR *Françoise Berthoud*
CLIENT *The New York Times Maga*

CHENILLE SWIRL DRESS, $680, by

Kulinka. At Shere, 1001 Madison Avenue.

CHATEAU-STYLE IRON GATE, *custom-made by Randolph Marshall for Les Métalliers Champenois.*

ILLUSTRATIONS BY FRANCOIS BERTHOUD

73

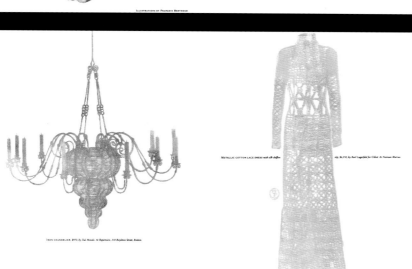

METALLIC COTTON LACE DRESS *with silk chiffon*

slip, $6,250, by Karl Lagerfeld for Chloé. At Neiman Marcus.

IRON CHANDELIER, $970, *by Owl Morale. At Repertoire, 218 Boylston Street, Boston.*

ILLUSTRATIONS BY FRANCOIS BERTHOUD

75

83 STEVEN BRILL

FOUNDER, CEO, COURT TV

◆ **LAST YEAR:** — ◆ **AGE:** 44 ◆ **CREDITS:** O.J. Simpson, the Bobbitts, the Menendez brothers, and the charm of highbrow scandalmongering have made this three-year-old cable station big business. ◆ **DEBITS:** Though Brill cashes in on the tabloid TV boom while savoring hard-news cachet, the rest of the media ape him like crazy, diluting his franchise.

84 RICHARD MOSK

CHAIRMAN, MPAA RATINGS BOARD

◆ **LAST YEAR:** — ◆ **AGE:** 54 ◆ **CREDITS:** Because an NC-17 rating can mean financial death, Hollywood's most powerful directors scramble to appease Mosk and his 10-member ratings board—giving them more power over final cut than any studio head. ◆ **DEBITS:** The MPAA continually gets dissed for being softer on violence than on sex.

85 HOWARD STERN

RADIO AND TV PERSONALITY

◆ **LAST YEAR:** — ◆ **AGE:** 40 ◆ **CREDITS:** Made over $40 million from his No. 1 book (soon to be a movie) *Private Parts*; has the clout to not get axed despite nearly $2 million in FCC obscenity fines. ◆ **DEBITS:** A late-night show for Fox was reportedly nixed after Murdoch saw his raunchy New Year's Eve special. Stern blames creative differences.

86 MEG RYAN

ACTRESS

◆ **LAST YEAR:** — ◆ **AGE:** 33 ◆ **CREDITS:** *When a Man Loves a Woman* not only confirmed her status as Hollywood's favorite romantic ingenue but expanded her range and could win her an Oscar nomination; will earn $8 million for her role in *The Women*. ◆ **DEBITS:** She's known for passing on high-profile films—*Maverick* being the most recent.

PORTRAIT BY HANOCH PIVEN

59

(facing page)
Distinctive Merit/National

FULL PAGE OR SPREAD
Howard Stern
ART DIRECTOR *Jill Armus*
CREATIVE DIRECTOR *Bob Newman*
DESIGNER *Jill Armus*
PHOTOGRAPHER *Monica Stevenson*
ILLUSTRATOR *Hanoch Piven*
CLIENT *Entertainment Weekly*

(above)
Distinctive Merit/International

FULL PAGE OR SPREAD
Strippers Hermengildo Sabat
ILLUSTRATOR *Seymour Chwast*
AGENCY *The Pushpin Group, Inc.*
CLIENT *Sección Aurea, Fundación Artes Visuales*

MERIT AWARDS

Merit/National

FULL PAGE OR SPREAD
Some Risk Doesn't Look Like Risk
ART DIRECTOR *Guy Marino*
DESIGNER *Guy Marino*
ILLUSTRATOR *Brad Holland*
CLIENT *Bankers Trust*

Merit/National

FULL PAGE OR SPREAD
Art Directors Club of Cincinnati Poster
ILLUSTRATOR *Brad Holland*
CLIENT *Art Directors Club of Cincinnati*

Merit/National

FULL PAGE OR SPREAD
Lucia di Lammer Moor
ART DIRECTOR *Jan Obye*
CREATIVE DIRECTOR *Ann Murphy*
DESIGNER *Rafal Olbinski*
ILLUSTRATOR *Rafal Olbinski*
AGENCY *Nappi-Eliran-Murphy*
CLIENT *New York City Opera*

BY JAY MARTEL

On "The Larry Sanders Show," Garry Shandling turns the talk-show brouhaha into the funniest thing on TV

>>> Ideally, the first sentence of an article about Garry Shandling would set a provocative scene – such as Shandling calling his co-workers "fucking idiots" – before settling down to the more mundane details about the life of a self-referential comedian and sometime talk-show host, the same Garry Shandling who played a self-possessed comedian on the TV show *It's Garry Shandling's Show* and who now plays a self-

absorbed TV talk-show host on the TV show *The Larry Sanders Show*, the same 44-year-old television auteur who has managed to turn selfness into a new TV form, the *narcissitcom*, without being self-indulgent and is now taking his act to the movies. But now it's too late. >>>

Merit/National

FULL PAGE OR SPREAD
Garry Shandling
CREATIVE DIRECTOR *Fred Woodward*
DESIGNERS *Fred Woodward, Gail Anderson*
ILLUSTRATOR *Robert Risko*
CLIENT *Rolling Stone*

HOW TO GIVE
ORDERS
LIKE A MAN

BY DEBORAH TANNEN

Merit/National

FULL PAGE OR SPREAD
How to Give Orders Like a Man
ART DIRECTOR *Janet Froelich*
DESIGNER *Nancy Harris*
ILLUSTRATOR *Gary Baseman*
CLIENT *The New York Times Magazine*

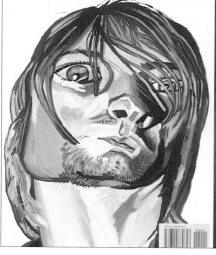

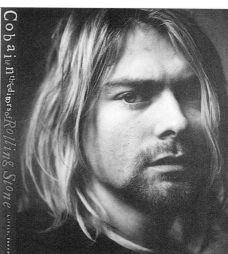

Merit/National

FULL PAGE OR SPREAD
Kurt Cobain
CREATIVE DIRECTOR *Fred Woodward*
DESIGNER *Fred Woodward*
ILLUSTRATOR *Philip Burke*
CLIENT *Rolling Stone*

KEEPING TIME BY JOHN SAYLES

A FICTION

THE OWNER ISN'T AROUND, so there is only an old man to help Mike with his kit. Each time Mike hands him another case from the van, he examines it, then nods and goes "Uh-huh" as if he's taking inventory. The old man is lanky, with maple-colored skin and eyes huge and soft behind thick lenses.

"Got to deal with the mess," he says when it's all inside and leaves Mike to set up alone.

The kit is pretty simple these days. Only two rack toms, floor tom, couple cymbals, the kick he just bought and the snare he's had forever. Mike looks to the back of the room where the old man is cleaning. The distance throws his time off, a gap between the push of the broom and the sweeping sound. Mike tightens the head on the snare. Need the firepower.

It is a club he hasn't played before, though *club* is an exaggeration. A former Grange hall with a makeshift bar, plywood sheet laid on shipping pallets for a stage. The stage is against the wall, which is better acoustics and always makes Mike feel more secure. The time outdoors in the storm with Blood Source, tumbling back into the ooze below the bandstand, neither the players in front nor the rain-soaked headbangers in the field noticed he was gone till his solo came up.

He's played worse.

If the janitor doesn't stick around for the first set, he'll be the oldest person in the club. Bet on it. The last show, keeping time under the new girl's vocal and looking out at the children in their torn clothes, washed in the red light, it sat on him hard.

The time he was keeping brought a picture to him, like it always did. This time he was breaking rocks on a chain gang, not a soulful, swinging, Sam Cooke kind of scene but something nasty and tired where each heavy-armed chop was another day off his life. It sat on him hard and heavy, and he looked out at the kids in the red light and thought, "Am I boring them, or are they boring me?"

"Man, you were buried in that groove tonight!" said Joey at the motel later. "Thought we'd have to call 911."

And later still, the phone call to his kid on the coast, the long stretches of dead air between them that Mike wanted to fill with drumming, screaming, something. "If it's too loud, you're too old," said the kid at the mixer board who'd kept creeping the volume up all night.

There was a time he'd be wired already, adrenaline pumping, just setting the kit up. Attack mode. Show time. Standing on the edge, waiting for the music to give him a nudge.

Mike's hands lay palm down on his thighs, dead meat.

The janitor comes up with a full dustpan to dump in a cardboard box next to the stage. He smiles at Mike.

"Mr. Time," he says, eyes flicking over the pieces of the drum kit. "Mr. Rhythm."

The old man chuckles to himself as he turns back

Though JOHN SAYLES is best known as an independent filmmaker ("Return of the Secaucus 7," "Eight Men Out," "Passion Fish"), he is also the author of three novels ("Union Dues," "Pride of the Bimbos," "Los Gusanos") and a collection of short stories ("The Anarchists' Convention").

48 · ROLLING STONE, DECEMBER 9, 1993

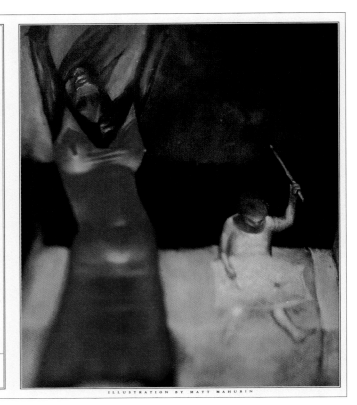

ILLUSTRATION BY MATT MAHURIN

Merit/National

FULL PAGE OR SPREAD
Keeping Time
CREATIVE DIRECTOR *Fred Woodward*
DESIGNER *Fred Woodward*
ILLUSTRATOR *Matt Mahurin*
CLIENT *Rolling Stone*

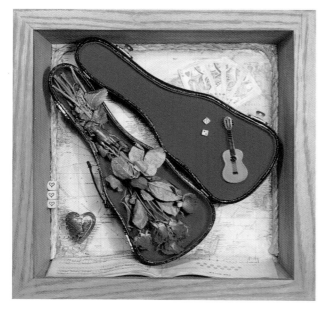

Merit/National

SERIES
VH1 Honors Awards
ART DIRECTOR *Cheri Dorr*
CREATIVE DIRECTOR *Cheri Dorr*
PHOTOGRAPHER *Lee Friedman*
ILLUSTRATOR *Melissa Meier*
PRODUCTION STUDIO *Robert Du Grenier Associates,*
New York
CLIENT *VH1*

Honey, They Shrunk the Planet. As communication and travel increasingly shorten the cultural distance from here to there, we find less and less reason to separate the National and International judgings. Instead, this year's Advertising and Graphic Design juries were drawn from both the United States and abroad, and each jury judged both the national and international work in its own discipline.

It is no small achievement to have one's work in this Art Directors Annual. The 74th National/9th International Annual Exhibition has been much praised as the strongest and best-looking show in years, and every winner in this book earned its place.

On the editorial side, we have taken great pains to present the winning work with elegance, clarity, and as much accuracy as humanly possible. The work deserves it.

—Myrna Davis
Executive Director, The Art Directors Club

1995 Recipients

Cooper Union
Robert Rindler, Dean

Michael Essl
Kaming Liu

F.I.T.
Jerry McDaniel, Chairperson

Erez Bahar
John Lamacchia
Chau Nguyen
Lisa Schofield

New York City Technical College
Joel Mason, Dept. Chairperson

Guy Champagne
Densford Jones
Tarunashwari Singh

Parsons School of Design
William Bevington, Dept. Chairperson

Parolio Matos
David Noboa
Liza Pagano
Gladys Yue

Pratt Institute
Joseph Roberts, Dept. Chairperson

Michael Kelly
Seungyun Je
Erik Ringerud
James Allan Spahr

Pratt Manhattan
Elliott Gordon, Dept. Chairperson

Bimo Pamungkas
Rie Shibayama

School of Visual Arts
Richard Wilde, Dept. Chairperson

Songju Hong
Robert Johnston
Terje Vist

1995 Donors

Roz Goldfarb
Walter Kaprielian
Ruth Lubell
The Art Directors Club, Inc.

The Visual Communicators Education Fund, Inc. (VCEF) was founded by the members of the Art Directors Club to aid and encourage the development of talented students entering the profession of art direction. It awards scholarship funds annually to advertising and design schools, who then designate the students who are to share them. Seven schools in the metropolitan area, listed opposite, were invited to participate this year. Department heads from each school selected the most deserving students entering their senior year of studies.

It was heartwarming to see the twenty-two student recipients gather at the Club for the award presentation, anticipating their names being called as their families and friends stood proudly by their sides. The evening served as an opportunity for the students to interact and for the department chairs to get to know each other or reminisce.

In recent years, one dollar from every entry into the Annual Exhibition has gone to the VCEF, and art auctions have been organized to which members and friends have contributed. All contributions to the VCEF are tax-deductible. The VCEF is planning new fund-raising activities for 1996. Our goal is to collaborate with more ADC members, to develop ideas and implement the ones we can to help aspiring art students fulfill their dreams.

—Richard MacFarlane
President, Visual Communicators Education Fund

United States

Aarons, Lawrence
Adamec, Donald
Adamek, Tina
Adams, Gaylord
Adams, Steven
Addiss, Patricia
Adelman, Jim
Adler, Peter
Adorney, Charles S.
Ahlgrim, Dennis
Allen, Heidi Flynn
Anderson, Jack
Anderson, Joseph
Andreasen, Susan
Andreozzi, Gennaro
Angeloni, Rick
Aragaki, Phyllis
Armario, David
Armour, Lawrence
Arnold, Stephanie A.
Aronson, Herman
Arthur, Rochelle L.
Babitz, Jeff
Bach, Robert O.
Badrinath, Arati S.
Baer, Charles H.
Baer, Priscilla
Baker, Eric
Ballister, Ronald
Barber, Ray
Barker, Floyd
Baron, Richard M.
Barrett, Christine
Barrett, Elizabeth A.
Barrios, Juan Jose Tejeda
Barron, Don
Barthelmes, Robert
Barton, Gladys
Bauch, Nancy
Baumann, Mary K.
Beaven, Clifford J.
Beaver, Allan
Beckman, Arthur
Bender, Lois
Bennett, Edward J.
Bennett, George
Benson, Laurence Key
Berenter, Bill
Berg, John
Berger, Danielle
Berman, Matt
Bernard, Walter L.
Bertolami, Peter
Bertulis, Frank
Best, Robert
Bevington, William
Beylerian, George
Binzen, Barbara
Blank, Janet
Blank, Peter J.
Blattner, Robert
Blechman, R. O.
Blend, Robert H.
Bloch, Bruce
Block, David S.
Bloom, Karen M.
Blumberg, Arnold
Bluming, Joel
Boches, Edward

Bode, Robert
Bodenschatz, Sharon
Bonavita, Donna
Booth, George Warren
Bourges, Jean
Bowman, Harold A.
Boyd, Doug
Brady, Evelyn M.
Braguin, Simeon
Brauer, Fred J.
Braverman, Al
Brent, Michael
Breslin, Lynn Dreese
Brockmeier, Bill
Brodsky, Ed
Brody, Ruth
Brody, Sam
Brooks, Adrienne
Brower, Steven
Brown, Beverly
Brown, George
Brown, Mark Delane
Bruce, Robert
Brugnatelli, Bruno E.
Brumberg, Gary
Buckley, William H.
Burkhardt, Ron
Butler, Bonnie
Bynum, Peter
Cadge, Bill
Canniff, Bryan G.
Caporimo, James
Cardillo, James
Carew, Bob
Carnase, Michael
Carnase, Thomas
Carruthers, Roy
Casado, Ralph
Cason, Merrill
Cassell, Emmett
Castelli, Angelo
Catherines, Diana
Ceradini, David
Cernero, Tina
Chambers, Jean
Chang, Andrew
Chaplinsky, Anthony, Jr.
Chen, Jack C.
Chermayeff, Ivan
Cherry, John
Chester, Laurie
Chetter, Shirley E.
Christie, Alan
Church, Stanley
Chwast, Seymour
Clapps, John
Clark, Alice
Clark, Herbert H.
Clarke, Bud
Clarke, James V.
Clemente, Thomas F.
Cline, Mahlon
Cohen, Joel
Cohen, Peter
Coll, Michael
Conner, Elaine
Connors, Catherine
Cook, M. Deidre
Cooper, David A.
Corey, Lee

Costabel, Eva
Cotler, Sheldon
Cotler-Block, Susan
Coverdale, Jac
Cox, Phyllis Richmond
Cox, Robert
Craig, James Edward
Crane, Meg
Crane, Susan J.
Cronan, Michael
Crossley, Gregory
Crozier, Bob
Cullen, Leslie
Cumbie, James Ty
Curry, Allison Davis
Curry, Christine
Cutler, Ethel R.
Cutshaw, Gregory F.
Davidian, David
Davidson, Steven
Davis, Barbara Vaughn
Davis, David R.
Davis, Paul B.
Davis, Philip
Davis, Randi B.
Davis, Theodore M.
Defrin, Bob
DeGregorio, Tony
Del Sorbo, Joe
DeMartino, Erick
Demoney, Jerry
Derderan, Thomas
Deutsch, David
DeVito, Frank
Dignam, John
DiVincenzo, Dennis
Doppelt, Shelley
Dorfsman, Louis
Dorian, Marc
Douglas, Kay Elizabeth
Drace, Matthew
Drenttel, William
Drucker, Rina
Dubiel, Ann
Duffy, Donald H.
Dunn, Faith
Eckstein, Bernard
Edgar, Peter
Edwards, Geoffrey T.
Eidel, Zeneth
Eisenman, Nina
Eisenman, Stanley
Eisner, Robert
Ellis, Judith
Endewelt, Jack
Epstein, David
Epstein, Lee
Ericson, Shirley
Ermoyan, Suren
Fable, Kathleen Quinn
Factor, Ellen
Fama, Joseph
Fanno, George
Fedele, Gene
Federico, Gene
Fenga, Michael
Ferrell, John
Filson, Kristin
Finelli, Douglas
Fink, Len

Fiorentino, Lou
Fiorenza, Blanche
Fischer, Carl
Fletcher, Patricia
Flock, Donald P.
Fraioli, John
Frankfurt, Stephen O.
Franklin, Richard
Freeland, Bill
Freyss, Christina
Friedland, Ruby Miye
Friedman, Beverly
Frith, Michael K.
Frost, Oren
Fuchs, Aaron
Fujita, Neil
Fury, Leonard W.
Gable, Mark A.
Gabrich, Michelle
Gaeta, Raymond
Gage, Robert
Galioto, Rosemarie
Gallo, Danielle
Gardner, Bert
Gardner, Hope
Garlanda, Gino
Gavasci, Alberto Paolo
Geissbuhler, Steff
Gennarelli, Charles
Genova, Gerald J.
George, Jeffrey E.
George, Robert J.
Geranmayeh, Vida
Germakian, Michael
Geryak, John
Gessman, Carl
Gialleonardo, Victor
Gibson, Kurt
Ginsberg, Frank C.
Giovanitti, Sara
Giraldi, Bob
Glaser, Milton
Gleason, Maureen R.
Gluckman, Eric
Gobe, Marc
Goen, Tama Alexandrine
Goettel, Manfred
Gold, Bill
Goldberg, Irwin
Goldfarb, Roz
Goldsmith, Gary
Goodfellow, Joanne
Goodman, Lee
Goss, Jeff
Govoni, Jean
Grace, Roy
Greiss, Abe S.
Greiss, Adam
Gribben, Chip
Griffin, Jack
Griffith, Jeffrey
Groglio, Glen P.
Growick, Phillip
Grube, Susan
Grubshteyn, Raisa
Grunther, Ira Alan
Gruppo, Nelson
Guerre, Kimberly
Guild, S. Rollins
Guzman, George

Hack, Robert
Hagel, Bob
Haiman, Kurt
Halvorsen, Everett
Hama, Sho
Hamilton, Edward
Hamilton, Frances M.
Hammond, Francis
Haney, David
Harris, Cabell
Hartwell, Alan
Hassel, Barry
Hayes, Connie
Heit, Amy
Heller, Steven
Hendricks, William
Hensley, Randall
Herche, Maureen
Hess, Jannike
Hill, Chris
Hillsman, William G.
Hirsch, Peter
Hively, Charles
Hoashi, Jitsuo
Hochhalter, Gordon
Hoffenberg, Harvey
Hoffmann, Nancy
Hoffner, Marilyn
Holland, Barry K.
Holtz, Jennifer
Horn, Steve
Horowitz, Julia L.
Houser, William David
Howard, Paul
Hoyt, Debra Morton
Huang, David
Hurd, Jud
Hutter, Brian
Incorvaia, Vito
Ishii, Skip K.
Jablonski, Andrew
Jacobs, Harry
Jaffe, Holly
Jaffee, Lee Ann
Jalbert, Ted
Jamison, John E.
Janerka, Andrzej
Jerina, Patricia
Jervis, Paul
Johnston, Shaun
Jones, Karen C.
Jubert, Joanne
Kalayjian, Vasken
Kalish, Nicki
Kanai, Kiyoshi
Kaprielian, Walter
Kaufman, Paul
Kay, Norman S.
Keane, Ronan J.
Keens, Elizabeth A.
Kelly, Brian M.
Kenny, Alice
Kent, Nancy
Kenzer, Myron W.
Keyton, Jeffrey
Khalifa, Jana
Kiel, Ronald
Kier, Ellen Sue
Kim, Bok-Young
Kim, Hyeson

Klein, Hedy
Klein, Judith
Klyde, Hilda Stanger
Kner, Andrew
Knier, Maria
Knoepfler, Henry O.
Koepke, Gary
Kohler, Denis
Komai, Ray
Korpijaakko, Kati
Krauss, Oscar
Kurz, Anna
La Barge, Robert
Lafferty-Dimmick, Christine
La Marca, Howard
Lamarque, Abril
Landi, Joseph O.
Lanotte, Michael
La Petri, Anthony
La Rochelle, Lisa A.
Larstanna, Lawrence
Lassi, Mark
Lau, Pearl
Lavey, Kenneth H.
Lawrence, Marie Christine
Lazzarotti, Sal
Lebeck, Steven W.
Lebron, Michael A.
Lee, Ching
Lee, David
Lee, Edwin
Le Van, Donna Lee
LeVesque, Shawn
Levine, Peter
Levine, Rick
Liberman, Alexander
Lloyd, Douglas
Lois, George
Lopez, Antonio
Lott, George
Lowry, Alfred
Lubell, Ruth
Lucci, John
Luger, Diane
Luna, Dennis Lopez
Luria, Robert
Lurin, Larry
Lyon, Robert W., Jr.
Lyons, Michael J.
MacFarlane, Richard
MacInnes, David H.
Magdoff, Samuel
Magnani, Lou
Mancino, Anthony
Mann, Edward Marc
Manser, Pamela G.
Marcellino, Jean
Marcus, Eric
Margolis, David R.
Mariucci, Jack
Marquez, Andrea
Mason, Joel
Mayer, Susan
Mayhew, Marce
Mazzeo, Joan
Mazzeo, Michael
McCaffery, William
McErlain, Stephen J.
McGreevy, Nick
Mednick, Scott A.

Meher, Karen L.
Meher, Nancy A.
Merkley, Parry
Metzdorf, Lyle
Metzner, Jeffrey
Meyer, Jackie Merri
Meyers, Kimberly
Meyn, Robbie
Miano, Thomas A.
Milbauer, Eugene
Miller, Larry
Milligan, John
Minor, Wendell
Miranda, Michael
Mitsch, Steven
Mizerek, Leonard
Mizrahi, Marise
Modenstein, Sam
Mok, Clement
Montebello, Joseph
Montone, Ken
Moore, Diane
Moore, Richard
Moore, Robert
Moran, Paul
Morita, Minoru
Morooka, Mami
Morris, Ann
Morris, Leonard
Morrison, William R.
Morton, Amy
Morton, Thomas
Moses, Louie
Moss, Tobias
Moyer, Dale
Mueller, Robert
Murphy-Hamill, Virginia
Nelson, Daniel
Nessim, Barbara
Newman, Robert
Newman, Susan
Nichols, Mary Ann
Nichols, Raymond
Nicolas, Serres Cousine
Nissen, Joseph
Nix, Michael
Noether, Evelyn C.
Norman, Barbara J.
Noszagh, George
November, David
Oberlander, Bill
Occipinti, Sharon
O'Donnell, Lisa
Okladek, John
O'Neill, Hugh
Ortiz, Jose Luis
Oswald, Mindy
Ovryn, Nina
Owett, Bernard S.
Paccione, Onofrio
Paganucci, Robert
Palancio, John A.
Palecek, Jane
Paley, Valerie Ritter
Pallas, Brad
Panetta, Susan
Pappalardo, Jeff
Park, James
Parker, Jacques
Pascoe, Kathleen

Paul, Art
Pedersen, B. Martin
Peduto, Patrick
Peeri, Ariel
Perone, Christopher C.
Perrotti, Tony
Perry, Harold A.
Perry, Roberta
Peslak, Victoria I.
Peter, John
Peterson, Christos
Petrocelli, Robert
Petrone, Chris
Petrucelli, Daniel
Pettus, Theodore D.
Phelps, Steward
Philiba, Allan
Phillips, James
Phipps, Alma
Pilla, Michael
Pioppo, Ernest
Pliskin, Robert
Portner, Richard
Posen, Frances
Pozsonyi, Anthony
Procida, Robert
Quackenbush, Michael
Queener, Charles W.
Querze, Elissa
Raboy, Dick
Rand, Paul
Reed, Samuel
Reeks, Deck P.
Reid, Kendrick
Reinke, Herbert
Reitman, Harris
Reitzfeld, Robert
Renaud, Joseph Leslie
Reshen, Amber
Reshen, Patricia J.
Rhodes, David
Richards, Stan
Richert, Ruthann
Rietschel, Barbara
Riley, Elizabeth T.
Ritter, Arthur
Ritter-Mayer, Karen
Roberts, Barbara B.
Roberts, Kenneth
Robinson, Bennett
Rockwell, Harlow
Rodney, Drew Ann
Rohall, Susan
Romano, Andy
Rosenthal, Bobbi
Rosner, Charlie
Rosner, Eric
Ross, Andrew
Ross, Mark
Ross, Peter
Ross, Richard J.
Rossiello, Suzanna M.
Roston, Arnold
Roth, Tom
Rothrock, Salleigh
Rothstein, Bette
Rottenberg, Eta
Rousseau, Ann Marie
Rowe, Alan
Rubenstein, Mort

Rubin, Randee
Rubinsky, Shelley
Ruis, Thomas P.
Russell, Henry N.
Russo, Albert
Russo, Deborah
Ruther, Don
Ruzicka, Thomas
Sachs, Joseph
Sacklow, Stewart
Saido, Tatsuhiro
Saito, Moriyoshi
Saks, Robert
Sala, Loretta M.
Saladino, Peter
Salcer, Richard M.
Salpeter, Robert
Salser, James
Saltz, Ina
Samerjan, George
Sauer, Hans
Sayles, John
Saylor, David J.
Scali, Sam
Scarfone, Ernest
Schaefer, Peter J.
Schenk, Roland
Scher, Paula
Schermer, Susan
Scheuer, Glenn
Schmalz, Paul
Schmidt, Klaus F.
Schnaufer, Joyce
Schrager-Laise, Beverly
Schrijver, Robert W.
Schultz, Eileen Hedy
Schultz, Kate
Schwartz, Adriane
Schwartzman, Julie
Scocozza, Victor
Scott, Robert A.
Sculco, Georgina
Seabrook, Alexis
Seabrook, William, III
Sears, Amy
Segal, Leslie
Segerstrom-Sato, Rebecca
Seidler, Sheldon
Seisser, Tod
Sellers, John L.
Shachnow, Audrey
Shafer, Franci
Silverstein, Heidi K. Eckman
Silverstein, Louis
Simmons, Robert
Simpson, Milt
Singer, Leslie
Sirowitz, Leonard
Sisman, Lucy
Skolnik, Jack
Smith, Carol Lynn
Smith, Robert S.
Smith, Sheila
Smith, Virginia
Sobel, Edward
Sokol, Andrew
Solomon, Martin
Solsburg, Mark
Sosnow, Harold
Spangler, Lee

Spears, Harvey
Spegman, Jim
Stackell, Isaac
Stamatopoulos, Nancy
Stansfield, Shelly Laroche
Stanton, Mindy Phelps
Stapelfeldt, Karsten
Stefanides, Dean
Steigelman, Robert
Steinbrenner, Karl
Steiner, Vera
Stern, Barrie
Stewart, Gerald
Stone, Bernard
Storch, Otto
Storrs, Lizabeth
Strizver, Ilene
Strosahl, William
Sugiura, Shunsaku
Sullivan, Pamela
Sullivan, Sharon
Suth, Pat
Sutton, David
Sweeny, Ken
Sweet, Leslie A.
Tansman, Jo Ann
Tartaglia, Frank
Tasch, Alex
Taschetti, Vincent
Tashian, Melcon
Taubin, William
Tauss, Jack G.
Tekushan, Mark
Tenne, George
Thalasinos, Nell
Thomas, Steve
Thompson, Bradbury
Todd, Robert
Toland, Toni
Tora, Shinichiro
Torzecua, Marlena
Towners, John C.
Trasoff, Victor
Trowbridge, Susan B.
Tsiavos, Anastasios
Tully, Joseph P.
Twomey, John D.
Udell, Rochelle
Ultimo, Clare
Urrutia, Frank
Vasquez, George
Verdia, Haydee N.
Viggiano, Jeanne
Vischo-Gallagher, Amy
Vitale, Frank A.
Vogler, David L.
Volpe, Maria Laurenzi
Von Schreiber, Barbara
Vornberger, Cal
Vuong, Thuy
Wachtenheim, Dorothy
Wajdowicz, Jurek
Wallace, Joseph O.
Walsh, Linda
Warren, Allison
Wasserman, Kenneth
Waxberg, Larry
Weber, Denise A.
Weber, Jessica
Weber, Peter

Weinheim, Donna
Weisel, Mimi
Weithas, Art
West, Robert Shaw
Wiedling, Daphne
Wilde, Richard
Williams, Rodney C.
Witalis, Rupert
Wittenburg, Ross
Wolf, Henry
Wolf, Jay Michael
Wollner, Michael Kjell
Wong, Nelson
Wong, Robert H.
Woods, Laura
Woodward, Fred
Yoffe, Ira
Yonkovig, Zen
Young, Frank
Young, Shawn
Zabowski, Bill
Zaino, Carmile S.
Zanis, Leo
Zator, Lynette Marie
Zeitsoff, Elaine
Zhukov, Maxim
Zielinski, Mikael T.
Zlotnick, Bernie
Zollinger, Lisa A.
Zuzzolo, Richard J.
Zwiebel, Alan

Australia
Dilanchian,
  Katheryn Davidian
Kambourian, Ron
Lee, Lisa

Austria
Demner, Mariusz Jan
Klein, Helmut
Lammerhuber, Lois
Merlicek, Franz

Belgium
Behaeghel, Julien
Lemaitre, Pascal

Bermuda
Smith, Paul

Brazil
Lima, Beto
Miranda, Oswaldo
Petit, Fransesc
Rampazzo, Adeir

Canada
Davidson, Rob
Pepin, Pierre
Tolpin, Larry

Czech Republic
Jasanska, Lenka

Denmark
Simonsson, Dres Simon

Germany
Arke, Rainer
Baier, Mario
Gross, Frank
Hebe, Reiner
Koch, Claus
Kuge, Claus
Leu, Olaf
Mojen, Friederike
Mojen, Ingo
Nebl, Lothar
Platt, Stephan
Pospischill, Hans-Georg
Prommer, Helga
Todd, Samy J.
Weber, Njoschi

Greece
Konstantinidis, Vangelis

Hong Kong
Chan, Elman
Cheung, Eddy
Chuen, Tommy Li Wing
Jacobs, Byron
McCudden, Colleen

India
Pereira, Brendan

Iran
Alikhani, Iraj Mirza
Rezaei, Ladan

Israel
Reisinger, Dan

Italy
Guidone, Silvano
Pavone, Gerardo
Stoppini, Luca

Japan
Akiyama, Takashi
Aoba, Masuteru
Aotani, Hiroyuki
Asaba, Katsumi
Baba, Yuji
Brenoe, Peter
Fukushima, Takenobu
Furumura, Osamu
Hirai, Akio
Ichihashi, Ken
Ito, Yasuyuki
Iwaki, Michio
Iwata, Toshio
Izumiya, Masaaki
Kamijyo, Takahisa
Kaneko, Hideyuki
Kashimoto, Satoji
Katsui, Mitsuo
Kawamoto, Fumio
Kitazawa, Takashi
Kojima, Ryohei
Kotani, Mitsuhiko
Maeda, Kazuki
Matsui, Keizo
Matsumoto, Arata
Matsumoto, Takaharu
Matsumoto, Takao

Matsunaga, Shin
Matsuura, Iwao
Miyasaka, Kuniaki
Mizutani, Koji
Morimoto, Junichi
Nagatomo, Keisuke
Nakahara, Michio
Nakahara, Yasuharu
Nakamura, Makoto
Oba, Yoshimi
Ohama, Yoshitomo
Ohashi, Toshiyuki
Ohtaka, Takeshi
Okada, Syuji
Okamoto, Shigeo
Okuizumi, Motoaki
Okumura, Akio
Okura, Kyoji
Omori, Shigeshi
Oseko, Nobumitsu
Saito, Toshiki
Sakamoto, Hiroki
Sakamoto, Ken
Suzuki, Yasuo
Suzuki, Zempaku
Takahama, Yutaka
Takanokura, Yoshinori
Tanabe, Masakazu
Tanaka, Ikko
Tanaka, Soji George
Tomita, Ben
Tomoeda, Yusaku
Uejo, Norio
Usami, Michihiro
Watanabe, Masato
Watanabe, Yosiko
Yamamoto, Akihiro H.
Yamamoto, Yoji

Korea
Ahn, Dan
Chae, Ki Young
Chang, Don Ryun
Chung, Joon
Chung, Joy
Han, Kwang Soo
Hwang, Jung Suk
Jang, Jung Hak
Kang, Yeong-Joon
Kim, Chul Han
Kim, Doo Hwang
Kim, Duk Kyu
Kim, Een Seok
Kim, Hae Kyung
Kim, Hyun
Kim, Kwang Kyu
Kwon, Hyun Chang
Lee, Jae Chul
Paik, Nack Mi
Park, Dong Hee
Park, Seung Soon
Park, Woo Duk
Rhee, Sang-Chol
Seo, Woon Suk
Sohn, Hye-Won
Yoon, Woong Jin

Malaysia
Ho, Veronica
Hoi, Tatsun
Lee, Yee Ser Angie
Wong, Peter

Mexico
Beltran, Felix
Flores, Luis Efren Ramirez

Monaco
Turello, Amedeo M.

The Netherlands
Brattinga, Pieter
Dovianus, Joep
Van Lotringen, Walter

Philippines
Abrera, Emily A.

Portugal
Aires, Eduardo

Singapore
Aitchison, Jim
Eng, Chiet-Hsuen

Spain
Folch, Jose M. Trias

Switzerland
Dallenbach, Bilal
Bundi, Stephan
Jaggi, Moritz
Kueste, Helmut
Schuetz, Dominique
Syz, Hans G.
Welti, Philipp

United Kingdom
Baker, Jim
Stothard, Celia

YOUR BRUSH. OUR PALETTE.
STEVENS PRESS, NYC 212·581·7470

CQ406ARER01 CM B 16-MAR-94 13:14 ROCH EMPIRE GRAPHICS CON. 133L

In Heaven, the Art Directors live on iced cappuccino and bon-bons in astounding oceanfront villas. Copywriters have wide, flat heads on which to set beverages. And everybody else has to jump through hoops all day long.

How to arrive

K O D A K

at the proof.

Okay, snap out of it. It's still the nineties and you've still got too much work, too little time. ♦ Kodak knows what you're dealing with these days. They've been inside photography and the graphic arts longer than anybody. So they know what you go through to get an idea from the shoot to the printed page. And they know how to get you there with products from films to plates, digital cameras to proofing systems. Kodak products at every point of the imaging chain, connected by Kodak's color science. Seamlessly. Beautifully. ♦ There are those of us who would probably change places with Fifi the circus poodle. And, in fact, do much better with their 401K.

Cara Galowitz *is the Manager of Graphic Design Services at the Guggenheim Museum, where she designs exhibition catalogues, retail posters, ephemera, interior and exterior signage, and graphics for exhibitions. Galowitz recently received a first prize award from the American Association of Museums for designing the publication* Art of This Century: The Guggenheim Museum and Its Collection.

After graduating from Cooper Union and prior to working at the Guggenheim Museum, Galowitz designed the logo, signage, stationery, publications, and ephemera for the Museum of the City of New York and The Brooklyn Public Library.

Woody Pirtle *ran his own graphic-design practice in Dallas for ten years before joining Pentagram in New York as a partner in 1988. Earlier, he worked at The Richards Group and studied architecture and fine art at the University of Arkansas. His logotypes, posters, environmental graphics, and corporate communications are often published as examples of the best of their kind.*

Pirtle's work is in the permanent collections of the Museum of Modern Art and Cooper-Hewitt National Design Museum in New York, the Neue Sammlung Museum in Munich, and the Zurich Poster Museum. He has taught at the School of Visual Arts, is a member of the Alliance Graphique Internationale, and has served on the boards of the magazine HOW *and the American Institute of Graphic Arts.*